Components of Successful Private Independent Catholic School Start-Ups in the United States.

The results of a dissertation completed by
Denise L. Donohue Ed.D.

Published by CreateSpace
ISBN 978-1502567871

Table of Contents

Figures

Preface

This research focused on four major components of successful private independent Catholic schools in the United States who were members of the National Association of Private Catholic* and Independent Schools (NAPC*IS) to determine the impact of the components on the successful start-up and sustainability of the schools. The major components were: (a) the individual, (b) the start-up process, (c) organizational decisions made at start-up, and (d) the operational environment in which the school opened. Success was measured by continued operation beyond the average closure rate of inactive member schools of 6.14 years. Areas of entrepreneurship and their application to NAPC*IS schools were explored.

Both active member schools open beyond 6.14 years and inactive schools were surveyed and the major components and sub-components within each major category were correlated. Results showed that individuals with a minimum of four years or more of college, who have previous supervisory experience and little financial investment in the new venture, and who built up the job flexibility and involvement of their teachers in strategies and goal setting of the school, characterized the lead entrepreneur or founder of the successful schools. Successful schools used the first three phases of the program planning model, planned a minimum of 22 weeks before opening, and operated with only formal written communication with the local Bishop. Standard operating procedures correlated significantly with longevity for both open and closed schools.

The research methodology, results, and discussion are being included in this booklet to assist those interested in opening up a private independent Catholic school. Additional school consulting services are available at the Cardinal Newman Society at www.cardinalnewmansociety.org.

Chapter 1: Introduction

The number of private Catholic independent schools has steadily increased over the last 40 years as recorded by the National Association of Private Catholic and Independent Schools (NAPC*IS). NAPC*IS, a membership and accrediting association, has a current membership of 58 active independent Catholic schools and is the only identifiable association in the United States that specifically exists to act as a resource and support for these schools. At the time when diocesan and religious order schools were losing enrollment and closing (McDonald & Schultz, 2011), these "lay-run" schools were opening. These schools are privately incorporated institutions operating in the United States whose founders and administers are not ordained religious, but lay-members of the Catholic Church. The earliest known independent Catholic school dates back to the early 1970s.

Topic

Currently there are 49.4 million school children in the United States. Of these 49.4 million students, 5.9 million of them have parents who have chosen to remove them from the government run system (U.S. Department of Education, National Center for Education Statistics [USDOE-NCES], 2011a). These families have chosen, for various reasons, to send their children to privately run schools. Of these privately run schools, the Catholic school system has been one of our nation's largest systems educating just over 2 million elementary and secondary school students (McDonald & Schultz, 2011). Catholic education has served as many as 5.2 million students annually during its peak period of operation in the 1960s, but over the past 40 years enrollment in those schools has faced a steady decline (McDonald & Schultz, 2011). In 2012–2013, charter schools in the country will, for the first time, enroll more private school students than Catholic schools (Kennedy, 2012).

As enrollment in Catholic schools declined, membership of NAPC*IS schools over the same time period has steadily increased (see Table 1), although small in number when compared to the Catholic school systems nationwide. The researcher, who volunteers as a NAPC*IS resource coordinator, continues to receive phone calls requesting assistance with opening small faith-based schools using a Catholic curriculum. While the NAPC*IS membership has grown to 107 schools since it first organized in 1995, 43 member schools have closed after an average of 6.14 years in operation, and 6 have dropped their membership but remain open. These six schools are not included in the active membership list used within this research project and are not considered part of the closed school group. These six schools have remained open and have either joined with the local diocesan school system or have joined with another accrediting agency. For the 43 schools that closed, this writer would like to know what research-based components might be put in place prior to opening that would help these schools remain open and viable for longer periods of time. Specifically, these research-based components would consist of the four main areas investigated in this project: (a) Qualities of the individual school founder, (b) start-up procedures used, (c) organizational decisions made, and (d) the local operational environment that consists of surrounding faith-based schools as well as the relationship with the local diocese and bishop.

Table 1

NAPC*IS Member Schools in Operation

Years	1970–1980	1990–1995	1996–2000	2001–2005	2006–2011
Number of schools	7	19	32	46	58

Note. The data for this table were obtained from Eileen Cubanski, Executive Director, NAPC*IS.

Overview of the Research Problem

This proposed study will investigate NAPC*IS schools in greater detail and specifically seek to uncover the components that have aided the opening of new member schools, that have helped them remain open, and that have helped to sustain existing member schools. While all the schools utilize a basic education framework, other factors such as being civilly incorporated and operating as nonprofit corporations "on the fringe" of the institutional Catholic Church might also be areas of concern for those individuals contemplating opening up a school.

This 40-year growth spurt of private independent "Catholic" schools is a fairly recent phenomenon in comparison to the history of the Catholic school system in the United States, which dates back to the early 1600s (National Catholic Education Association, 2011). It is a phenomenon because the growth and constancy of such schools is not well understood or documented. It is an oxymoron because traditionally Catholic schools have been organized and administered under the authority of a bishop in a diocese and run by a superintendent of schools. Independent Catholic schools are organized and operated under a lay-led board of directors. Some lay-run schools have been given the authority by the bishop to use the term "Catholic" in their title and operate as privately funded schools adhering to certain diocesan rules. Private independent Catholic schools are led by the laity of the Catholic Church who desire a faith-based, academic option for their children based upon the teachings of the Catholic Church with little to no relationship with the institutionalized Catholic Church.

A majority of the independent Catholic schools (54%) operate in the East Coast time zone (E. Cubanski, personal communication, December 27, 2011; NAPC*IS, 2013a). Twenty-one percent are located in the Central time zone. Fourteen percent are in the West Coast time zone; 9% are in the Mountain Standard time zone; and one school (2%) is in Alaska. There are a total of 58 current member NAPC*IS schools across the United States. Of those schools, 23% are K–12 schools, 17% are K–8 schools, 16% are PreK–8 schools, 17% are other combinations, and 9% each are PreK–12 schools, Grades 7–12 schools, and Grades 9–12 schools.

Statement of the Research Problem

The independent Catholic schools have operated and have grown steadily over the past 40 years in the United States, yet there is a 40% closure rate for NAPC*IS member schools (E. Cubanski, personal communication, December 27, 2011). Statistics on schools currently open are minimal and statistics on closed schools are sparse when looking at the data kept by NAPC*IS. The reasons why those schools closed are difficult to ascertain since once schools close many of the teachers, administrators, and founders move on and are hard to locate. This researcher attempted to contact all of the NAPC*IS closed schools by their last registered email, website address, or listed phone numbers with minimal results and was able to generate a streamlined list of school contact information. It would be helpful to those contemplating opening a school to know what components influenced the successful start up and eventual sustainability of those schools. In essence, what are the necessary components in the area of the individual founder or entrepreneur, necessary start-up procedures, early organizational decisions and environment, that aid in a successful start-up and sustained operation of an independent Catholic school? How can those who desire to open such schools be served?

Recent statistics from NAPC*IS indicated that the beginning of this movement consisted of one school. Today there are 58 member schools (see Table 1). NAPC*IS member schools are only a small fragment of a movement that has an estimated 180 identified schools nationwide (E. Cubanski, personal communication, March 31, 2007). Of the 107 schools who held active member status as NAPC*IS schools, 43 of the schools have closed after operating on average for 6.14 years (E. Cubanski, personal communication, December 27, 2011). The closed schools at one time comprised 40% of the total member schools of the organization. Additionally, eight of the schools never opened. The reasons for incorporating and opening independent Catholic schools vary. Many schools opened in the early 1970s because parents were dissatisfied with how the existing Catholic schools incorporated the teaching of human sexuality in their curriculum (E. Cubanski, personal communication, March 23, 2011). Other schools opened because existing Catholic schools were closing (McDonald & Schultz, 2011), and some schools opened because Catholic schools did not exist in their geographical area. As the reasons for opening independent Catholic schools vary, so too, are the reasons for the closure of some of these schools. From the membership roster of active and inactive or closed schools received from Eileen Cubanski, the Executive Director of NAPC*IS, a majority of schools closed due to a lack of enrollment or other financial constraints. Some schools closed because of governance or control issues (Guernsey & Barott, 2008). Having worked with these schools for 10 years, this researcher was never made aware of any type of formal feasibility studies that were performed prior to school openings. As a resource coordinator and prior independent school administrator, this researcher helped to provide those interested in opening a school with minimal guidance addressing questions such as how to go about the process of incorporating, resources for curriculum, and personnel qualifications. Formal feasibility study material, like some presented in this research, is not within NAPC*IS's sphere of available services. NAPC*IS does not have any research-based data, such as what this study hopes to obtain, currently available (E. Cubanski, personal conversation, November, 2012).

Deficiencies in the Evidence

Guernsey and Barott (2008) indicated that no previous research had been performed on the independent Catholic schools (p. 3). While there is an organization that has been formed (NAPC*IS) to unify and accredit the independent Catholic schools, those schools have basically existed without any formal research performed regarding their existence or operations. NAPC*IS began with a rudimentary and dated "start-up" manual which was anecdotal and site specific. It has revised its manual for online purposes, but still lacks any research-based data (NAPC*IS, 2013b) for justification of its suggested startup procedures, policies, or administrative recommendations.

Audience

This research study will provide information to prospective founders, administrators, and individuals interested in starting an independent Catholic school and those already operating an independent Catholic school. Potential investors and benefactors to those schools would be able to identify research-based components indicative of a successful and sustainable business venture. Diocesan superintendents and bishops who currently work with those schools, or who may potentially have schools opening up in their geographical boundaries, would also benefit from the additional research regarding this steadily growing trend and their relationship to the diocesan school system. Ultimately, this research is important to all those interested in the education of our nation's children.

Purpose of the Study

The purpose of this research study was to identify components in the area of the school founder, the start-up procedures used, the early organizational decisions made, and the environmental issues regarding the relationship with the bishop and his schools that influence the successful start-up and sustainability of NAPC*IS schools. This study focused on active and in-active NAPC*IS member schools located in the United States. It solicited responses from previously contacted school founders who have closed their schools, as well as school founders who were still operating their schools and who held active membership status. Only schools that had been in existence beyond the average closure age for inactive member schools of 6.14 years were solicited for this research. Schools open past the average closure rate of 6.14 years are considered to have had a successful start up, simply by the criterion that they are currently open. By identifying and verifying these important factors which are associated with the successful start-up and sustainability for current independent Catholic school membership, those individuals interested in starting a new private school in the Catholic tradition might use this information to make prudent and cost effective decisions.

Definition of Terms

Catholic schools. Catholic schools are those schools recognized by the institutional Catholic Church and recorded in the Official Catholic Directory. They may be considered parochial (controlled by a parish), diocesan (controlled by the diocese), or private (controlled by a recognized religious order or non-clerical board).
Components. In this research study, components included qualities and characteristics of the individual, the start-up process, the organization, and the environment as identified by Duchesneau (1987). Within these main categories were sub-components of education, experience, risk-taking, and personal financial commitment of

the individual founder; alternatives sought, time spent planning, inclusion of client base in project, market analysis used, professionals involved, and formal business plan developed for the start-up procedure; capacity of personnel, management system and evaluation used, leadership style, time on task, and utilization ratio of the beginning organization; and the relationship with the bishop, number of competing Catholic schools, percentage of Catholic students in the school, geographic location of the school, and stability of the school board for the environment.

Entrepreneur. This definition reflected the framework study by Duchesneau (1987) who took his definition for entrepreneur from Ronstadt (1984). It is
For purposes of this study, we define an entrepreneur as a person who is a primary force in starting, acquiring, or franchising a relatively new and independent organization for profit or non-profit purposes. Such person may not necessarily be the initial founder nor the sole entrepreneur associated with the venture. However, individuals who acquire by purchase or inheritance older or larger businesses with an established sales base are not included in this definition. Also excluded are persons who are 'internal' or corporate 'entrepreneurs' who may start new businesses while they are essentially employees of another organization. (Ronstadt, 1984, p. 437)

Founder. Wadhwa, Aggarwal, Holly, and Salkever (2009) defined founder as "an early employee, typically joining the company in its first year, before the company developed its products and perfected its business model" (p. 7). By using this definition, it leaves open the opportunity for those individuals who may not have a significant financial investment in the formation of a new school, or who are not incorporated board members, to respond to the survey.

Independent Catholic school. Guernsey and Barott (2008) defined an independent Catholic school as a "school that identifies itself (with a) Catholic vision of education but does not fully operate within the legal, financial, or administrative structures of the diocese or a religious order" (p. 2). There are some schools which operate in this fashion, but who have been given the authority by the local bishop to use the word "Catholic" in their title. While they would be categorized as "Catholic–Private" schools for governmental demographic purposes, these schools were considered independent Catholic Schools within this paper. The use of the word "Catholic" in "independent Catholic school" as used within this paper does not connote approval by the local bishop of these schools, just that they have chosen a Catholic vision for their educational framework.

NAPC*IS. This is an acronym for the National Association of Private Catholic and Independent Schools. The asterisk has a footnote referencing the fact that some of these schools are approved by the local bishop and may use the word "Catholic" in their title. NAPC*IS does not, and cannot, bestow the use of that word to any school, nor claims that it can do so.

Success. In order to identify components of successful schools, the term "success" was defined. Since the premise of this research is to identify components of success for schools that have remained open after the average closure age of 6.14 years, "success" was defined as those schools that remained open and operating for 7 or more years.

Chapter 2: Methodology

This chapter will describe the participants of the study, the study design, the creation, modification, and determination of validity of the survey instrument, and the procedures for data collection and analysis. The methodology for this research was chosen based upon the questions this researcher wished to answer. Having worked with individuals interested in opening up independent schools, this researcher desired more quantitative data to better assist them rather than to rely upon personal experience or antidotal discussions. Since this is an understudied field, rich with numerous variables that might influence the success of a new start-up organization, this researcher chose to use an observational, explanatory design to uncover and correlate components that might, or could, effect a successful and sustainable educational entity.

In order to reach all of the NAPC*IS founders of schools throughout the United States, this researcher chose to use both electronic and hardcopy surveys to collect information from these schools. This researcher had direct access to the NAPC*IS school membership list of both active and inactive members and was kept updated of new members by the organization's executive director.

Participants

The entire number of schools operating as independent Catholic schools in the nation is unknown. An official national directory for independent Catholic schools does not exist. NAPC*IS is the only national association with an official membership directory which lists schools operating exclusively in this fashion. Many schools that are not members of NAPC*IS apply to other nonsectarian, local, or regional accrediting agencies for affiliation and membership support. Others may operate without affiliation to any other organization. Some privately incorporated schools have received the ability to use the word "Catholic" in their title by their bishop and are listed in the Official National Catholic Directory. Those schools may also be associated with state, regional, and local accrediting agencies. Because of the lack of a national membership directory for all schools operating in this manner, the membership list of active schools associated with NAPC*IS was reviewed as the target population. In addition to these schools, all inactive member schools were included as part of the target sample. The unit of analysis was the school as opposed to the individual school founder or the environment. The study uncovered components about the school as an organization, the founder as the head of the school, the start-up procedures used and the school's relationship to the bishop. The characteristics of the schools included the fact that they were all privately incorporated and governed by a group of lay people; all taught the Catholic faith as an integral part of the curriculum; all participated in the reception of the sacraments of the Catholic church; all were predominately financed by tuition, fundraising, and development efforts; all were run by a headmaster or principal; and all were college-preparatory, or classical as opposed to vocational and technical schools.

NAPC*IS schools. From the target population of all active NAPC*IS schools, only those schools who had been in operation over the average closure rate for closed NAPC*IS schools (7 years) were sent a general letter, both by email and postal mail, soliciting interest in participation in the study (see Appendix B). All schools that respond were included in the study. Those who viewed the invitation electronically and chose to participate were immediately directed to the electronic survey link. Those who chose to participate using a hard copy were mailed a hard copy survey by postal mail. All schools that were currently open 7 years and beyond were believed to have some components of success and were eligible for inclusion in the study. Of the 43 closed NAPC*IS member schools, it was hoped that at least a minimum of five schools would response to the survey request.

Internal and external considerations. A list of internal and external considerations and outcomes were identified for this study (see Figure 1). What was interesting to note was how the philanthropic funding affected the activities of the school leader or founder in areas such as risk-taking and personal financial commitment (Section 1.1).

Schools	Internal Considerations	External Considerations	Outcomes
Open Schools 7years or more	**1.1 The Individual:** • Formal Education • Small business experience • Leadership experience • Entrepreneurial experience • Personal risk-taking • Personal financial commitment • Full-time experience in education field	Significant "bankrolling" of start-up school	Success
Closed schools	**1.2 Start-Up Procedure:** • Market analysis performed? • Alternatives & options sought? • Time spent planning • Inclusion of client base in project? • Professionals involved? • Formal business plan and/or notes?	Significant "bankrolling" of start-up school	Success
	1.3 The Organization: • Capacity of personnel • Management: systems & evaluations • Leadership Style • Time on Task • Utilization Ratio	Outside philanthropic funding as a percentage of school budget	Success
	1.4 The Environment: • Relationship with the Bishop • Number of competing Catholic schools. • Stability of school board		Success

Figure 1. Study design.

Chapter 3: Results

This chapter reports the survey results received from school founders and administrators of NAPC*IS schools. These results are reported by the components studied in the survey of (a) the Individual, (b) the Start-Up procedures used, (c) the Organizational decisions made upon start-up, and (d) the Environment at start-up. The results of the subcomponents of education, experience, risk-taking, and personal financial commitment of the individual founder, alternatives sought, time spent planning, inclusion of client base in project, market analysis used, professionals involved, and formal business plan developed for the start-up procedure; capacity of personnel management system and evaluation used, leadership style, time on task, and utilization ratio of the beginning organization; and the relationship with the bishop, number of competing Catholic schools, percentage of Catholic students in the school, geographic location of the school, and stability of the school board for the environment are reported by the components of open and closed schools. These results are also reported by the two variables of open and closed schools, where the open schools are considered the successful schools and the closed schools are the unsuccessful schools. Success, as defined in this study, is the existence of those schools open and operating for 7 or more years.

Research Questions

The following four questions guided this explanatory research design to uncover and correlate components that might, or could, affect a successful and sustainable educational entity. They are:

1. What are the critical qualities and characteristics of the school founder that lend to a successful start-up and sustainability of an independent Catholic school?

2. What are the critical issues and components that must be addressed in the start-up process of opening an independent Catholic school?

3. What are the essential early organizational decisions and strategies that will aid in the success of a new independent Catholic school?

4. How does the relationship with the bishop and geographic location of the independent school affect its success?

The Sample

The sample included 58 NAPC*IS member schools in geographical locations across the country. Of the 46 open schools in the sample, 26 were located in the eastern time zone, 8 were located in the central time zone, 8 were located in the Pacific time zone, 3 were in the mountain time zone, and 1 school was in Alaska. Of the 12 responding schools from the sample, 6 were in the eastern time zone, 3 were in the Pacific time zone, 2 in the central time zone, and 1 in the mountain time zone.

The oldest member school in the target sample was in operation for 42 years. The youngest member schools in the target sample have been in operation for 8 years. There were no member schools in operation for 7 years, which is the designated number of years for successful schools as defined in this study.

Of the 58 NAPC*IS member schools in the target population, 46 of these schools are currently open and 12 of them have closed. Of the total of 43 previously closed NAPC*IS member schools, only 12 schools had emails or mailing addresses where individuals could be contacted. Of these 12 closed school contacts, 5 of them responded to the survey. This is 41.67 % return for closed schools with emails or post office mailing addresses or 11.62 % of the total number of closed member schools. Of the 46 open schools in the target sample, 12 of the schools responded to the survey. This is 26% of the target membership of eligible open schools.

Descriptive Statistics

As a non-experimental, observatory and explanatory study, this is a first-time effort (E. Cubanski, personal communication, April 9, 2014) to glean large amounts of quantifiable data from an association of schools who, for the most part, have chosen to operate independently of the recognized diocesan Catholic school structure. Because of the relatively small amount of survey responses, nonparametric statistics were used for inferential reporting. It is perhaps more important to look at the descriptive statistics to view a nascent picture of the types of individuals who found these schools, the critical issues and organizational decisions they make at start-up, and their relationship to the existing diocesan school structure than to search for probable predictive relationships within such a small sample. Therefore, the majority of data reported is in the descriptive format.

The Individual

Founders of open schools have had substantial previous full-time work experience with 41.67% reporting they had worked between 6 or more years in the field of education before opening their school (see Table 2). Twenty-five percent report having worked 16 or more years in education before opening their school. Eighty percent of the founders or lead administrators of closed schools had between 1-10 years of full-time work experience in education prior to opening the school and 20% had no previous full-time experience in the field of education. No founders or administrators in closed schools worked full-time in education longer than 10 years prior to opening up their school.

Table 2

Full-Time Work Experience in Education

Years experience	Open (N = 12)		Closed (N = 5)	
	N	%	N	%
None	3	25.0	1	20.0
1-5 years	4	33.3	2	40.0
6-10 years	1	8.3	2	40.0
11-15 years	1	8.3	0	0.0
16 years or more	3	25.0	0	0.0

Fifty-eight percent of the open school founders had previous supervisory experience supervising between 3 and 200 employees (see Table 3). Closed school founders had experience supervising between 0-50 employees prior to opening their schools. No closed school founders supervised more than 50 employees.

Table 3

Largest Number of People Supervised

People supervised	Open (N = 12)		Closed (N = 5)	
	N	%	N	%
0-2	5	41.7	2	40.0
3-10	2	16.7	2	40.0
11-50	1	8.3	0	0.0
51-250	4	33.3	0	0.0

Eighty-three percent of the open school founders have small business experience (41.67%, 16 years or more, 41.67%, 1 to 5 years; see Table 4). Only 16.7% reported not having any precious small business work experience. Closed school founders reported that 20% had no small business experience prior to starting the school, 40% had between 1–5 years of previous small business experience, and 40% had 16 or more years of small business experience before opening the schools. None of the founders of closed schools reported having between 6-15 years of small business experience.

Table 4

Previous Years Worked in Small Business

Years experience	Open (N = 12)		Closed (N = 5)	
	N	%	N	%
None	2	16.7	1	20.0
1-5 years	5	41.7	2	40.0
6-10 years	0	0.0	0	0.0
11-15 years	0	0.0	0	0.0
16 years or more	5	41.7	2	40.0

One open school founder reported opening more than seven small businesses and represents the most experienced small business entrepreneur of the reporting group (8.3% of open schools) (see Table 5). Interestingly, 50% report never having previously opened a business and 41.67% reported opening between one to two businesses. Closed schools founders report having had little previous experience opening other businesses with 40% never opening other businesses and 60% opening between one to two other businesses. No one reported opening more than two businesses.

The majority of open school founders reported having experienced little to no personal risk upon opening the school with 50% reporting their personal investment was under $1,000 (see Table 6). Sixty percent of closed school founders reported having "some" to "great" personal risk and 40% reported "small" to "none" personal risk. None of the founders felt their risk was catastrophic.

Table 5

Previous Start-Up Experience

Business started	Open (N = 12)		Closed (N = 5)	
	N	%	N	%
0	6	50.0	2	40.0
1-2	5	41.7	3	60.0
3-4	0	0.0	0	0.0
5-6	0	0.0	0	0.0
7 or more	1	8.3	0	0.0

Table 6

Perception of Personal Risk

Perception of risk	Open (N = 12)		Closed (N = 5)	
	N	%	N	%
None or practically none	5	41.7	1	20.0
Small	4	33.3	1	20.0
Some	1	8.3	2	40.0
Great	2	16.7	1	20.0
Catastrophic	0	0.0	0	0.0

Sixty percent also had a slight investment in the school between $1,001-20,000, with 20% reporting between $0-1,000 invested in the school operations from personal savings or borrowing (see Table 7). Twenty percent also reported having between $20,001–40,000 of personal contributions invested in the school operations. No one reported contributions to the school in excess of $40,001.

Table 7

Personal Investment

Dollars invested	Open (N = 12)		Closed (N = 5)	
	N	%	N	%
$0-1,000	6	50.0	1	20.0
$1,001-20,000	4	33.3	3	60.0
$20,001-40,000	0	0.0	1	20.0
$40,001-60,000	0	0.0	0	0.0
$60,001 or more	2	16.7	0	0.0

The founders of the open schools all reported holding a minimum of 4 years of college, a master's degree, or a doctoral degree (see Table 8). There were no founders with less than a 4-year graduate degree or only a high school background in the open school group. Eighty percent of the closed school respondents had 4 or more years of college, with 20% having between 1-3 years of college completed (see Table 8). No closed school founders had doctoral degrees.

Table 8

Highest Level of Education

Level of education	Open (N = 12)		Closed (N = 5)	
	N	%	N	%
High school or less	0	0.0	0	0.0
1–3 Years of college	0	0.0	1	20.0
4 Years of college	5	41.7	2	40.0
Master's degree	5	41.7	2	40.0
Doctoral degree	2	16.7	0	0.0

To characterize the founders or lead administrators of open schools, one would say they are academically astute individuals with significant experience supervising others in both education and small business operations. They have little personal investment tied up in the new school endeavor and see little to no personal risk if the school failed. Characterizing the closed school founder is difficult because of the limited sample, but from the gathered data one can say that the founder has some previous full-time experience in education (11-10 years), some small business experience (1-5 years or 16 or more), and some previous supervisory experience (40% with 0 to 2 employees and 60% between 3 and 50 employees). These founders have a moderate investment in the school (i.e., between $0-40,000) and feel personally responsible if the school fails. For the most part they have 4-year college or master's degrees (80%).

The Start-Up Procedure

Almost the entire group of open schools received only between $0-50,000 at start-up (see Table 9). Compared with the closed schools that all reported having received between $0–50,000 from outside sources at opening, the open schools had one school reporting that they received over $200,001 prior to start-up (see Table 9). No schools, open or closed, received between $50,001-200,000 in outside source funding prior to start-up.

Almost 92% of open schools had some contact or substantial contact or market analysis with potential families prior to start-up (see Table 10), yet only 41.7% report their written notes addressed their client base (see Table 12). Sixty percent of the closed schools noted covering their client base in their written notes or business plan (see Table 12). One hundred percent of the closed schools reported having some contact with potential families or market analysis performed at start-up.

Table 9

Funding Received by Outside Source at Start-Up

Money received	Open (N = 12)		Closed (N = 5)	
	N	%	N	%
$0–50,000	11	91.7	5	100.0
$50,001–100,000	0	0.0	0	0.0
$100,001–150,000	0	0.0	0	0.0
$150,001–200,000	0	0.0	0	0.0
$200,001 or more	1	8.3	0	0.0

Table 10

Market Analysis and Potential Families

Contact analysis	Open (N = 12)		Closed (N = 5)	
	N	%	N	%
No contact-analysis	0	0.0	0	0.0
Very small-limited	1	8.3	0	0.0
Some contact	9	75.0	5	100.0
Substantial contact	2	16.7	0	0.0
Extensive-	0	0.0	0	0.0
Comprehensive				

Both the open and closed schools indicated that they did not exhaust searching for alternatives ways and means to opening a new school by indicating that 0% sought "A great number." It was only in the open schools did 8.3% seek "Substantial" alternative ways and means to address schooling. The closed schools did not seek alternative ways and means to this level, but 40% did seek "Some alternative" ways and means to address the need compared to the open schools where 33.3% sought "Some alternative" ways and means. Both the open and closed schools indicated with a 58.3% and 60% respective response that very few or limited alternatives and means were sought.

Table 11

Alternative Ways and Means Explored

Ways and means	Open (N = 12)		Closed (N = 5)	
	N	%	N	%
No alternative	4	33.3	2	40.0
Very few-limited	3	25.0	1	20.0
Some alternative	4	33.3	2	40.0
Substantial	1	8.3	0	0.0
A great number	0	0.0	0	0.0

What is interesting to note in the areas covered in the business plan or written notes (see Table 12) is that all of the closed schools identified their financial need and possible resources as well as their facility needs and resources in their written note or business plan, whereas only 66.7% of the open schools addressed these areas. One would think that these areas would be a primary concern for all individuals or organizations undertaking a new venture. We know that at least one open school identified substantial financial resources received prior to opening (see Table 9). We can only speculate if the other open schools who received between $0-50,000 were on the high end of that level (toward $50,000) and felt comfortable to proceed without planning for addressing the need of seeking additional financial resources, or even facility and space needs as addressed by the low percentage (66.7%) who included these areas in their written notes or financial plan. Incorporation notes were identified in both groups at about the same rate (83% for open schools and 80% for closed schools). All schools in the target population must receive incorporation to operate. Both open and closed schools indicated equity in the pre-planning use of financial statements that included an income statement and a balance sheet (41.7% for open schools and 40% for closed schools), and both open and closed schools showed near equal planning for personnel (66.7% for open schools and 60% or closed schools). Another item of interest is the fact that open schools indicated more pre-planning for their organizational design (75%) versus the closed schools that indicated only 40% detailed their organizational design during start-up.

Table 12

Areas Covered in Business Plan or Notes

Business plan areas	Open (N = 12)		Closed (N = 5)	
	N	%	N	%
Incorporation	10	83.3	4	80.0
Marketing	5	41.7	3	60.0
Financial needs and resources	8	66.7	5	100.0
Balance sheet & income stmt	5	41.7	2	40.0
Facility needs & resources	8	66.7	5	100.0
Personnel needs	8	66.7	3	60.0
Organizational design	9	75.0	2	40.0

There seems to be a dichotomy concerning the involvement of potential families during start-up between the open and closed schools (see Table 13). The open schools indicate only 33% of potential families as being "Substantially Involved" and 25% being involved to some degree. Almost 42% of the open schools indicated that there was "Not at all" or "A Little" bit of involvement by potential families. This is in comparison to the closed schools that involved potential families by a total of 80%, with 60% "Substantially Involved" and 20% "Greatly Involved." None of the open schools indicated potential families were in the "Greatly Involved" category.

Table 13

Potential Families Involved in Start-Up

Degree of involvement	Open (N = 12)		Closed (N = 5)	
	N	%	N	%
Not at all	2	16.7	0	0.0
A little	3	25.0	1	20.0
To some degree	3	25.0	0	0.0
Substantially involved	4	33.3	3	60.0
Greatly involved	0	0.0	1	20.0

The average number of weeks prior to start-up was 28 weeks or 7 months for open schools (see Table 14). Approximately 38 hours per week went toward school planning and start-up efforts. The total reported average hours of work put into the project before opening was reported by open schools to average 783 hours. Not all respondents answered how many hours per week or total hours per week were spent planning for the open schools. The closed schools reported an average of 34 weeks spent planning for the school at 24 hours per week for a total on average of 534 as reported by the respondents.

In both the open schools and closed schools the involvement of professionals to assist with the start-up fell mostly between the "A Little" category and "Substantially Involved" category with 91.6% for the open schools and 100% for the closed schools (see Table 15). Only one school reported no involvement of other professionals in the business plan in the open schools. Neither the open or closed schools reported any professional involvement in the highest category of "Greatly Involved."

Table 14

Weeks, Hours Spent Planning for School Start-Up

Time spent planning	Open (N = 12)		Closed (N = 5)	
	N	%	N	%
Number of weeks	12	28.0	5	34.0
Hours per week	10	38.0	5	24.0
Total number of hours	10	783.0	5	534.0

Table 15

Degree of Professional Involvement in Business Plan

Degree of professional involvement	Open (N = 12)		Closed (N = 5)	
	N	%	N	%
Not at all	1	8.3	0	0.0
A little	4	33.3	1	20.0
To some degree	4	33.3	3	60.0
Substantially involved	3	25.0	1	20.0
Greatly involved	0	0.0	0	0.0

An attorney was used the most by the open and closed schools (see Table 16) compared to other professionals (see Table 17, Table 18, Table 19). The open schools used an attorney 26.7% more than the closed schools. An attorney would have been used for writing up the incorporation documents and, possibly, making sure the school's name is available for use in the geographic area.

Table 16

Use of an Attorney

Use of an attorney	Open (N = 12)		Closed (N = 5)	
	N	%	N	%
No	4	33.3	3	60.0
Yes	8	67.3	2	40.0

Both the open and closed schools reported that for the most part they did not use an accountant. Seventy-five percent of open schools and 80% of closed schools reported that these services were not procured. Generally, an accountant would prepare income statements and balance sheets for companies as well as forecasting budgets. More open schools than closed schools used an accountant.

Table 17

Use of an Accountant

Use of an accountant	Open (N = 12)		Closed (N = 5)	
	N	%	N	%
No	9	75.0	4	80.0
Yes	3	25.0	1	20.0

For the most part, the open and closed school both indicated that they did not use a banker for start-up assistance. Seventy-five percent reported "No" for open schools and 80% reported "No" for closed schools respectively (see Table 18). A banker would have been used to procure a business loan for the new venture.

The open and closed schools also indicated that they did not use an architect for start-up assistance. Seventy-five percent reported "No" for open schools and 80% reported "No" for closed schools (see Table 19). An architect's services would have been used for designing school facilities.

Table 18

Use of a Banker

Use of a banker	Open (N = 12)		Closed (N = 5)	
	N	%	N	%
No	9	75.0	4	80.0
Yes	3	25.0	1	20.0

Table 19

Use of an Architect

Use of an architect	Open (N = 12)		Closed (N = 5)	
	N	%	N	%
No	9	75.0	4	80.0
Yes	3	25.0	1	20.0

Also, both open and closed schools indicated that they used written notes (see Table 20) as opposed to the write up of a formal business plan (see Table 21). A majority of the open school (91.7%) used written notes and records. This was similar for the closed schools (80%).

Conversely, both open and closed schools indicated that they did not use a formal business plan prior to start-up. Seventy-five percent of open schools and 80% of closed schools reporting "No" for the use of a formal business plan (see Table 21). A formal business plan would have been used to seek financing for the new venture. Business plans are generally presented to bankers for loans and potential benefactors, business 'angels,' or foundations for grants.

Table 20

Use of Written Notes or Records for Start-Up

Use of written notes or records	Open (N = 12)		Closed (N = 5)	
	N	%	N	%
No	1	8.3	1	20.0
Yes	11	91.7	4	80.0

Table 21

Development of a Formal Business Plan Prior to Start-Up

Formal business plan prior to start-up	Open (N = 12)		Closed (N = 5)	
	N	%	N	%
No	9	75.0	4	80.0
Yes	3	25.0	1	20.0

Respondents from the open schools indicated that they sent their written business plans to at least one, and up to five, different people to review. Forty-one percent sent their written business plan to no one. From the closed school respondents, 60% indicated they sent their written business plan to no one and 40% sent their written business plan to at least one other person or five or more people.

To summarize the start-up procedures for open and closed schools: almost all the schools started with $50,000 or less having some degree of contact with their potential client base. Many schools indicated making the decision to open without seeking a substantial or a great number of other alternatives for education. Identification of financial needs and possible resources in written notes were important to a majority of all schools. More of the open schools indicated more pre-planning in their organizational design and involved potential families less. The average number of weeks before start-up for open schools was 28 weeks or 7 months at an average of 38 hours a week, or almost full-time. Professionals were used to some degree or not at all for both groups. A majority of both the open and closed schools used written notes or records for start-up instead of a formal business plan.

Table 22

Written Business Plans Sent to Individuals

Written business plans sent to individuals	Open (N = 12)		Closed (N = 5)	
	N	%	N	%
0 People	5	41.7	3	60.0
1 Person	1	8.3		20.0
2–3 People	5	41.7	0	0.0
4 People	0	0.0	0	0.0
5 or More people	1	8.3	1	20.0

The Organization

Both open and closed schools had approximately the same percentage of employees who were qualified to fill more than one position at the opening of the school (see Table 23), a similar percentage of the number of teachers involved in goal setting and strategies (see Table 31), the same percentage of administrators involved in work activities (see Table 33), a similar percentage of administrators who worked under 40 hours or fewer at another job the first year following start-up (see Table 37), but substantial differences existed between the two categories in other areas of organizational decision making. Those differences included the number of employees qualified to fill more than one position currently or at the closing of the school (see Table 24), the extent to which employees follow standard operating procedures and policies (see Table 25), the detail of these standardized operating procedures (see Table 26), the extent of performance appraisal procedures used for evaluation (see Table 27), having a single person in charge of the school (see Table 28), having board members in charge of decision making concerning goals and strategies (see Table 29), having administrators involved in decision making concerning goals and strategies (see Table 30), and the percentage of board members involved in work activities of the school (see Table 32).

In both the open and closed schools there were 66.7% and 60% respectively of employees unable to fill more than one position at the opening of the school. This question targets the capacity of the school's human resources to be flexible in moving employees into other organizational roles within the school on an as-needed basis. In this instance, both categories of schools reported little flexibility for employees at start-up to switch into other roles (see Table 23). Whereas, currently, or at the close of the school, open schools reported 75% of their employees were able to shift into other positions, compared to only 40% of the closed schools (see Table 24). Three open schools reported having employees who, at start-up, were able to fill more than one position. Forty percent of closed schools reported, "About half are qualified," or "Many are qualified."

Seventy-five percent of open schools reported having employees at closing who were capable of filling more than one position at the school (see Table 24). Closed schools reported similar percentages at closure as they did upon opening. Twenty-five percent of open schools reported "Few are qualified" at closing, whereas 60% of the closed schools reported "Few are qualified" at closing.

Table 23

Employee Flexibility at Opening

Employees able to fill more than one position	Open (N = 12)		Closed (N = 5)	
	N	%	N	%
None	0	0.0	1	20.0
Few are qualified	8	66.7	2	40.0
About half are qualified	1	8.3	1	20.0
Many are qualified	0	0.0	1	20.0
All or nearly all are qualified	3	25.0	0	0.0

Table 24

Employee Flexibility Today or at Closing

Employees able to fill more than one position	Open (N = 12)		Closed (N = 5)	
	N	%	N	%
None	0	0.0	0	0.0
Few are qualified	3	25.0	3	60.0
About half are qualified	3	25.0	1	20.0
Many are qualified	5	41.7	1	20.0
All or nearly all are qualified	1	8.3	0	0.0

One hundred percent of open schools reported that their employees follow standard operating procedure and policies to a substantial and great extent (see Table 25). Closed schools reported 60% in this same category and also that 40% followed standard operating procedures and policies only to some extent.

Table 25

Extent of Employee Adherence to Policy

Follow SOP and policies	Open (N = 12)		Closed (N = 5)	
	N	%	N	%
Not at all	0	0.0	0	0.0
To a small extent	0	0.0	0	0.0
To some extent	0	0.0	2	40.0
To a substantial extent	4	33.3	2	40.0
To a great extent	8	66.7	1	20.0

Seventy-five percent reported that these standard operating procedures and policies were "quite" to "very specific," whereas 40% of the closed schools reported their operating procedures and policies were "quite" to "very specific." Most of the closed schools (60%) indicated their operating procedures were somewhat specific and 25% of the open schools said their operating procedures were "Mostly General."

Table 26

Degree of Detail of Standardized Operating Procedures

Degree of detail of SOP	Open (N = 12)		Closed (N = 5)	
	N	%	N	%
Very general	0	0.0	0	0.0
Mostly general	3	25.0	0	0.0
Somewhat specific	0	0.0	3	60.0
Quite specific	5	41.7	1	20.0
Very specific	4	33.3	1	20.0

Open schools reported that 75% of them used performance appraisal procedures for evaluation to a "substantial" and "great extent," whereas closed schools used them to only 40%. Closed schools used performance appraisal procedures for evaluation to a small extent (60%) and open schools used them to a small extent at 25%.

Table 27

Extent of Performance or Appraisal Procedures Used for Evaluation

Extent of performance or appraisal procedures	Open (N = 12)		Closed (N = 5)	
	N	%	N	%
Not at all	0	0.0	0	0.0
To a small extent	3	25.0	3	60.0
To a substantial extent	4	33.3	1	20.0
To a great extent	5	41.7	1	20.0

Of the open schools, 91% indicated they had a single person in charge of the school to a "substantial" or "great extent" as compared to 60% of the closed schools (see Table 29). The closed schools reported that a single person was in charge only to a small extent (40%).

Table 28

Degree a Single Person is in Charge of the School

Single person in charge of school	Open (N = 12)		Closed (N = 5)	
	N	%	N	%
To no extent	0	0.0	0	0.0
To a small extent	1	8.3	2	40.0
To a substantial extent	5	41.7	1	20.0
To a great extent	6	50.0	2	40.0

Interestingly, 75% of the board members of the open schools were involved "quite a bit" and "very much" in establishing goals and strategies, whereas, overwhelmingly, 100% of the board members in the closed schools were involved in establishing goals and strategies. Twenty-five percent of open schools noted that board members were involved in decisions regarding goals and strategies only "a little."

Table 29

Board Members Allowed to Make Decisions on Goals and Strategies

Board members' decision making	Open (N = 12)		Closed (N = 5)	
	N	%	N	%
None	0	0.0	0	0.0
A little	3	25.0	0	0.0
Somewhat	0	0.0	0	0.0
Quite a bit	4	33.3	3	60.0
Very much	5	41.7	2	40.0

Again, we see a bit of a shift between the open and closed schools in the administrators' involvement in goals and strategies. The open schools involved the administrators "Quite a bit" and "Very Much" 91.6% of the time, whereas the closed school involved administrators "Quite a bit" and "Very Much" only 60% of the time (see Table 30). All administrators in both groups were involved in decision making regarding goals and strategies at least "somewhat" and no administrators were excluded completely from this area.

The teacher involvement in decision making regarding goals and strategies was about even for both groups at 83.3% for open schools and 80% for closed schools (see Table 31). The closed schools did not eliminate teacher involvement at all, whereas one school, or 8.3%, did.

Table 30

Administrators Allowed to Make Decisions on Goals and Strategies

Administrative decision making	Open (N = 12)		Closed (N = 5)	
	N	%	N	%
None	0	0.0	0	0.0
A little	0	0.0	0	0.0
Somewhat	1	8.3	2	40.0
Quite a bit	7	58.3	2	40.0
Very much	4	33.3	1	20.0

Table 31

Teachers Allowed to Make Decisions on Goals & Strategies

Teacher decision making	Open (N = 12)		Closed (N = 5)	
	N	%	N	%
None	1	8.3	0	0.0
A little	1	8.3	1	20.0
Somewhat	3	25.0	3	60.0
Quite a bit	7	58.3	1	20.0
Very much	0	0.0	0	0.0

Most interesting to note was the fact that in the open schools, board member activity in day-to-day work activities within the school were limited to "None" (25%) or "A Little" (41.6%) at a total of 66.7% (see Table 32). This is quite the opposite from closed schools whose board members were involved from "Somewhat" through "Quite a Bit" to "Very Much" at 80% of the time. Board members of open schools were only involved "Quite a bit" at 25% of the time and were involved "Very Much" (the highest category) 0%.

Table 32

Board Members Involved in Making Decisions on School Work Activities

Board members' decisions on school activities	Open (N = 12)		Closed (N = 5)	
	N	%	N	%
None	3	25.0	0	0.0
A little	5	41.7	1	20.0
Somewhat	1	8.3	2	40.0
Quite a bit	3	25.0	1	20.0
Very much	0	0.0	1	20.0

Both administrators in open schools and administrators in closed schools were involved from "Somewhat" to "Very Much" in the day-to-day work activities of the school (see Table 33). Each category indicated a total of 100% response in these graduated categories. No administrators were eliminated from these activities or only showed "A Little" involvement.

Table 33

Administrators Involved in Making Decisions on School Work Activities

Administrators' decisions on school activities	Open (N = 12)		Closed (N = 5)	
	N	%	N	%
None	0	0.0	0	0.0
A little	0	0.0	0	0.0
Somewhat	1	8.3	2	40.0
Quite a bit	5	41.7	1	20.0
Very much	6	50.0	2	40.0

Also of interest to note is that teachers in the open schools were reported by one school to not be involved in the decision making of the day-to-day work activities in the open schools at 8.3%. Another open school reported that teachers were involved only "A Little" in the decision making of the day-to-day work activities at 8.3%. All other open schools reported that teachers were involved in decision making of work activities from "Somewhat" to "Very Much" at a total of 83.3% compared to a total of 100% of the closed schools in the same categories (see Table 34).

Table 34

Teachers Involved in Making Decisions on School Work Activities

Teachers' decisions on school activities	Open (N = 12)		Closed (N = 5)	
	N	%	N	%
None	1	8.3	0	0.0
A little	1	8.3	0	0.0
Somewhat	4	33.3	3	60.0
Quite a bit	3	25.0	1	20.0
Very much	3	25.0	1	20.0

In both the open and closed schools, lead founders reduced their total hours per week, worked at the opening of the school to the closing, or currently, at the school. At opening, 66.7% of the lead entrepreneur-founders reported working over 50 hours or more per week and 60% of the closed school lead entrepreneur-founders reported working over 50 hours per week at opening (see Table 35).

Table 35

Total Hours Lead Entrepreneur/Founder Worked During First Year of School

Hours worked	Open (N = 12)		Closed (N = 5)	
	N	%	N	%
40 Hours or fewer per week	4	33.3	1	20.0
40–50 Hours per week	0	0.0	1	20.0
50–60 Hours per Week	2	16.7	1	20.0
60–70 Hours per week	4	33.3	1	20.0
More than 70 hours per week	2	16.7	1	20.0

Both groups reduced their hours during the last 6 months of school with open schools indicating a more reduced amount at 41.7% and the closed schools at 60% (see Table 36). Working between 50-60 hours per week remained stable for both the open and closed groups. Working between 40-50 hours per week during the last 6 months increased by 25% for the open school founders.

Table 36

Total Hours Lead Entrepreneur/Founder Worked During Last 6 Months of School

Hours worked	Open (N = 12)		Closed (N = 5)	
	N	%	N	%
40 Hours or fewer per week	5	41.7	3	60.0
40–50 Hours per week	3	25.0	0	0.0
50–60 Hours per week	2	16.7	1	20.0
60–70 Hours per week	1	8.3	1	20.0
More than 70 hours per week	1	8.3	0	0.0

The majority of open and closed school entrepreneur/founders in both groups worked fewer than 40 hours at another job following the start-up of the school (see Table 37). There were, though, some individuals who worked at other jobs following the start-up of the school. Twenty-five percent of the open school entrepreneur/founders worked 40 hours or more at another job following start-up, and 40% of the closed school entrepreneur-founders worked at another job following start-up.

Table 37

Total Hours Lead Entrepreneur/Founder Worked at Another Job Following Start-Up

Hours worked	Open (N = 12)		Closed (N = 5)	
	N	%	N	%
40 Hours or fewer per week	9	75.0	4	80.0
40–50 Hours per week	1	8.3	0	0.0
50–60 Hours per week	1	8.3	1	20.0
60–70 Hours per week	0	0.0	0	0.0
More than 70 hours per week	1	8.3	0	0.0

Both open and closed schools received a majority of funds from outside sources between $0-50,000 during the last year of operation. Sixty-six percent of the open schools reported that during their last year (or last year of operation) they received between $0-50,000, and 80% of the closed schools reported receiving between $0-50,000 of income from outside sources (see Table 38). Two of the open schools reported receiving $200,001 and above during the last year from outside sources, and one received between $150,001 and $200,000 during the last year from outside sources. On the other hand, no closed schools reported receiving this much funding, although one school reported receiving between $50,001-100,000 in outside funds during its last year of operation.

Table 38

Funding From Outside Sources During Last Year or Last Year of Operations

Outside funding received	Open (N = 12)		Closed (N = 5)	
	N	%	N	%
$0–50,000	8	66.7	4	80.0
$50,001–100,000	1	8.3	1	20.0
$100,001–150,000	0	0.0	0	0.0
$150,001–$200,000	1	8.3	0	0.0
$200,001 or above	2	16.7	0	0.0

Eighty percent of the closed schools indicated at closing having an operating budget of $200,000 or less, whereas only 33.3% of open schools were operating at this level with 66.7% operating at $200,001 and above. Six of the open schools had budgets of $400,001 and above.

Table 39

Annual Operating Budget, Currently or During Last Year of Operations

Annual operating budget	Open (N = 12)		Closed (N = 5)	
	N	%	N	%
$0–100,000	1	8.3	2	40.0
$100,001–200,000	3	25.0	2	40.0
$200,001–300,000	2	16.7	1	20.0
$300,001–$400,000	0	0.0	0	0.0
$400,001 or above	6	50.0	0	0.0

Question 1.311 regarding the grade levels served by the schools indicated a high percentage choosing "Other Configuration" at 75% for open schools and 60% for closed schools (see Table 40). Of the open schools participating in the survey, three (25%) reported have a K-8 configuration.

Table 40

Grade Levels Served

Grade levels served	Open (N = 12)		Closed (N = 5)	
	N	%	N	%
K–6 or fewer grades	0	0.0	0	0.0
K–8	3	25.0	0	0.0
7–12	0	0.0	1	20.0
9–12	0	0.0	1	20.0
Other configurations	9	75.0	3	60.0

Because of the high percentage reporting they had "Other Configurations," more detailed information regarding these configurations was gleaned from the responses. This detail proved interesting in the sense that the open schools overwhelmingly showed an expansive school alignment of either Pre K-12 or K-12 (75%) (see Table 41). No other configurations, such as Pre K-6, or high school by itself was reported in the open schools, whereas in the closed school group two schools reported serving either 9-12 or 7-12. Even in the "Other Configuration" of the closed schools, two of those schools were K-12.

One hundred percent of the closed schools reported serving fewer than 50 students during their last month open; whereas only two open schools (16.7%) reported serving fewer than 50 students (see Table 42). Eighty-three percent of the open schools served more than 51 students with 41.7% reporting they served between 101–200 students.

Table 41

Other Grade Configurations

Grade configurations	Open (N = 12)		Closed (N = 5)	
	N	%	N	%
Pre K	0	0.0	1	20.0
Pre K–12	3	25.0	0	0.0
K–12	6	50.0	2	40.0
Other	3	25.0	2	40.0

Table 42

Students Served Currently or During Last Year of Operations

Students	Open (N = 12)		Closed (N = 5)	
	N	%	N	%
0–50	2	16.7	5	100.0
51–100	3	25.0	0	0.0
101–200	5	41.7	0	0.0
201–300	1	8.3	0	0.0
301 Above	1	8.3	0	0.0

According to O'Meara, Ferguson, Whelan, & Conway's (2012) findings, the actual enrollment compared to potential enrollment had an influence on the financial outcome of the school. Questions pertaining to how many students the school was serving (see Table 42) and to how many students the school was capable of serving were asked (see Table 43).

The open schools reported a higher average ratio of current students to maximal capacity of students at 72.5% (see Table 44). The ratio of current students served to maximal capacity of students served in the closed schools averaged 43.6%. This is a 28.9% difference in servicing ability. Also, the number of students that the open schools can serve averaged 178 students compared to the closed schools averaging student capacity of 59 students (see Table 44).

Table 43

Students Capable of Being Served Today or During Last Year of Operations

Students served	Open (N = 12)		Closed (N = 5)	
	N	%	N	%
0–50	1	8.3	1	20.0
51–100	3	25.0	4	80.0
101–200	5	41.7	0	0.0
201–300	1	8.3	0	0.0
301 Above	2	16.7	0	0.0

As defined by the categories, the open schools reporting information have all been open for 7 or more years. Almost 42% of them have been in operation just over 18 years and fewer than 24 years. One open school reported being open over 24 years. Conversely, 60% of the closed schools were open between just over 6 years and not more than 12 years. Forty percent of reporting closed schools were not open after 6 years.

Finally, the average operating time for closed schools who responded in this study was 35 months or 2 years and 11 months. The average number of months schools were in operation for the open schools is 200.42 months or 16 years and 8 months. The oldest open school in operation has been open for 312 months or 26 years and two of the youngest responding open schools have been in operation for 120 months or 10 years.

Table 44

Number of Students Being Served and Students Capable of Being Served

School	Open (N = 12)		Closed (N = 5)	
	N	%	N	%
1	11/20	55.0	15/35	43.0
2	386/530	90.0	24/60	40.0
3	195/210	93.0	45/100	45.0
4	187/200	94.0	15/50	30.0
5	293/350	84.0	30/50	60.0
6	110/200	55.0		
7	60/100	60.0		
8	30/75	40.0		
9	100/100	100.0		
10	58/180	32.0		
11	80/120	67.0		
12	152/152	100.0		

Table 45

Months School Open

Months (years)	Open (N = 12)		Closed (N = 5)	
	N	%	N	%
0-24 Months (2 years)	0	0.0	1	20.0
25-72 Months (6 years)	0	0.0	1	20.0
73-144 Months (12 years)	3	25.0	3	60.0
145-216 Months (18 years)	3	25.0	0	0.0
217-288 Months (24 years)	5	41.7	0	0.0
289 or More months	1	8.3	0	0.0

Table 46

Months School Open: Detail

School and months open	Open (N = 12)	Closed (N = 5)
	Months	Months
1	240	132.0
2	240	96.0
3	228	9.0
4	120	70.0
5	216	108.0
6	312	
7	120	
8	180	
9	141	
10	168	
11	200	
12	240	
Range	192	123.0
Mean	200.42	8.30
Standard deviation	57.28	47.01

The difference between the open and closed school categories are that open schools have more students (see Table 42) and an average higher ratio of student service capacity than closed schools (see Table 44). Open schools are receiving more money than closed schools (see Table 38) and have larger operating budgets (see Table 39). The configuration of open schools included mainly PreK-12th grade alignment, whereas two of the closed schools incorporated secondary schools. Administrator involvement in school decision making was strong in both open and closed schools (see Tables 30 and 33), whereas board members were more heavily involved in the work activities of closed schools as well as goal and strategy making. In open schools, board members seemed to concentrate more on setting goals and creating strategies. In open schools, the extent of a single person in charge of the school was more evident (91.7%; see Table 28) than the closed schools as well as the use of performance and appraisal procedures for evaluation (see Table 27). Both categories of schools indicated that the majority used standard operating procedures and policies.

The Environment

Three questions were used to gauge the relationship between the private independent Catholic schools and the bishop of the diocese. These questions were whether the bishop had formally recognized the schools as a Catholic school and allowed them to use the word "Catholic" in their title (Question 43), whether the diocese advertised the private independent Catholic school alongside the schools in its system (Question 44), and whether there was only formal written communication between the private independent school and the diocese (Question 45). These questions were chosen because of the experience of the researcher who operated a private, independent Catholic school and who worked through the process of being approved by the Diocese and being able to use the word "Catholic" in the school's title. When the diocese does not approve a school, generally there is only formal written communication between the private independent school and the diocese. When the private independent school has been approved, generally at some point within the relationship between the two entities there might be mutual advertising, promotion, and collaborative efforts. It is interesting to note that 58.3% of the open schools are not recognized by the bishop. One school that is recognized commented that it was only after 18 years of operating as an independent school that the bishop recognized them. This school is not included in the official Catholic directory, though. Only one of the closed schools was recognized by the diocese.

A review of the 46 open member schools on the NAPC*IS website showed only five schools stating they were officially recognized by their local bishop on their websites. Only one of these five schools responded to the survey. Four of the five surveyed schools did not indicate on their websites that the local bishop recognized them, yet they indicated in their response to Question 44 that this was the case. When one takes just the website information from each school to gather information regarding recognition by the local bishop, only five schools made mention of this out of the target sample of 46 open member schools. This is 20%. Adding the additional schools from the survey responses to those schools identified by their websites, this percentage moves up to 28%.

Table 47

School Recognized by Bishop as "Catholic" and in Catholic Directory

School recognized by bishop	Open (N = 12)		Closed (N = 5)	
	N	%	N	%
Yes	5	41.7	1	20.0
No	7	58.3	4	80.0

Thirty three percent of the open schools and 20% of the closed schools said the diocese includes their school with other diocesan schools in marketing advertisements. The majority of both open (66.7%) and closed (80%) schools are not included in diocesan advertising efforts (see Table 48).

Four of the open schools (33.3%) and one (20%) of the closed schools stated that only formal written communication existed between the diocese and the school. This might mean that either more or less communication existed between the school and the diocese.

Thirty three percent of the open schools indicated that between 6 and 10 diocesan elementary schools existed within 45 minutes of their school (see Table 50). Three schools indicated between 0-5. Two open schools indicated between 11 and 20 diocesan elementary schools within 45 minutes of their school. One open school reported more than 21 diocesan elementary schools within 45 minutes of their school. One school indicated "Several" and one school indicted "Many." Of the closed schools, three schools, or 60% said there were between "0-5" diocesan elementary schools within 45 minutes, and one school reported between "6-10" diocesan elementary schools. None of the closed schools indicated more than 11 diocesan elementary schools within 45 minutes of them, but one school indicated "several."

Table 48

Diocese Includes School in Diocesan and Other Advertisements

School in diocesan and other advertisements	Open (N = 12)		Closed (N = 5)	
	N	%	N	%
Yes	4	33.3	1	20.0
No	8	66.7	4	80.0

Table 49

Formal Written Communication Between Diocese and School

Diocese and school written	Open (N = 12)		Closed (N = 5)	
communication	N	%	N	%
Yes	4	33.3	1	20.0
No	8	66.7	4	80.0

Table 50

Number of Diocesan Elementary Schools Within 45 Minutes of School

Number of schools	Open (N = 12)		Closed (N = 5)	
	N	%	N	%
0–5	3	25.0	3	60.0
6–10	4	33.3	1	20.0
11–20	2	16.7	0	0.0
Above 21	1	8.3	0	0.0
Several	1	8.3	1	20.0
Many	1	8.3	0	0.0

One half of those administrators responding to the question regarding how many students attend diocesan elementary schools within 45 minutes of their school indicated they had no idea (Unknown) (see Table 51). Two open schools indicated between 1,000-2,500 students. Only two open schools indicated that there were fewer than 200 students attending these schools. Sixty percent of the closed schools indicated between 301–2,500 students attended the surrounding diocesan elementary schools.

Open schools reported more diocesan high schools within 45 minutes from their location with 50% indicating between 3-8 high schools within 45 minutes. Conversely, 80% of the closed schools reported that only between 0–2 high schools existed within 45 minutes of their school.

Eighty percent of the closed schools indicated that the number of students attending diocesan high schools within 45 minutes from their location was between 501 and 1,000 students. The open schools, again, had a large percent (41.7%) of respondents indicating they did not know the number of students in these schools (although more knew these schools existed as indicated from their response in Table 52).

Table 51

Number of Students Attending Diocesan Elementary Schools in Table 50

Number of students	Open (N = 12)		Closed (N = 5)	
	N	%	N	%
0-200	2	16.7	2	40.0
201-300	1	8.3	0	0.0
301-500	1	8.3	1	20.0
501-999	0	0	1	20.0
1,000-2,500	2	16.7	1	20.0
Unknown	6	50.0	0	0.0

Table 52

Number of Diocesan High Schools Within 45 Minutes of School

Number of schools	Open (N = 12)		Closed (N = 5)	
	N	%	N	%
0–2	5	41.7	4	80.0
3–5	4	33.3	1	20.0
6–8	2	16.7	0	0.0
Several	1	8.3	1	20.0

One hundred percent of the closed schools indicated their school board did not remain relatively stable, and 83.3% of open schools indicated their school board did not remain relatively stable. Only two open schools reported that their school board remained relatively stable.

Table 53

Number of Students Attending Diocesan High Schools in Table 52

Number of students	Open (N = 12)		Closed (N = 5)	
	N	%	N	%
0–100	1	8.3	1	20.0
101–500	2	16.6	0	0.0
501–1,000	1	8.3	4	80.0
1,001–2,000	1	16.6	0	0.0
Above 2,001	1	8.3	0	0.0
Unknown	5	41.7	0	0.0

Table 54

School Board Remained Relatively Stable

Stable school board	Open (N = 12)		Closed (N = 5)	
	N	%	N	%
No	10	83.3	5	100.0
Yes	2	16.7	0	0.0

Inferential Statistics

Because of the small sample size and the use of ordinal variables, the Spearman correlation was used to find correlations between targeted variables such as the founders' sense of personal risk and outside funding as well as their own personal investment and outside funding. This nonparametric statistic is warranted because of the lack of a normal distribution of the data. Both the .05 and .01 levels of significance were used. Correlations between selected other variables were performed to see if there was any relationship to longevity. All schools responding to the survey, both open and closed, were included in this analysis.

Although not statistically significant, there is some relationship according to Fink (2003) between the variables of personal risk and outside funding at start-up (.37). See Table 56. This is also true with the founders' personal investment and outside funding at start-up (.41). A moderate to good relationship is considered to be between .26 to .50 or -.26 to -.50 and a very good to excellent relationship would be between .51 to .75 or -.51 to -.75 (Fink, 2013).

Table 55

Spearman Correlations of Selected Questions With Personal Risk or Investment

Comparisons of correlations	Combined (N = 17)	
	r	p
Personal risk & outside funding at start-up	.37	.14
Personal risk & outside funding current/last year	−.38	.13
Personal investment & outside funding at start-up	.41	.10

*p< .05. **p < .01.

When using Spearman's Rho to correlate these same variables between the two groups of schools, only the closed schools indicated any type of correlation between the "Personal Risk and Outside Funding at Start-up" (.47) and "Personal Investment and Outside Funding at Start-up" (.48). The open schools did not even register a correlation between the variables in these two comparisons and there was little to no relationship (Fink, 2003) in the open school group between "Personal Risk and Outside Funding" during the current year.

Table 56

Spearman Correlations of Selected Questions With Personal Risk or Investment, Open and Closed Schools

Comparisons of correlations	Open (N = 12)		Closed (N = 5)	
	r	p	r	p
Personal risk & outside funding at start-up			.47	.13
Personal risk & outside funding current/last year	.18	.77	-.52	.08
Personal investment & outside funding at start-up			.48	.12

*p< .05. **p < .01.

It is warranted to include even the closed schools in the total sample when performing the Spearman Rho inferential statistic because the variables were measured against longevity, or length of time the school was open. Some of the closed schools responding to the survey were open past the average total of years used (6.14) to indicate success in this survey, and therefore might have some variables that correlate to success.

When looking at the selected variables from the survey (see Table 57), there are two correlations between the range of .26 and .50 (-.26 and -.50) that Fink (2003b) would label as fair. These are incorporation and longevity (.44) and organizational design and longevity (.47). The one statistically significant correlation ($p < .01$ level) is standard operating procedures and longevity (.61). Here, both open and closed schools indicated they used standard operating procedures at least to some extent and this correlated to their time in operation, or longevity. No other paired variables indicted a statistically significant correlation.

Table 57

Spearman Correlations of Selected Questions With Longevity Variable

Question	Combined (N = 17)	
	r	p
Full-time experience in education	.11	.66
Years worked in small business	−.04	.88
Prior business start-up	−.21	.42
Highest level of education	.25	.33
Number of weeks planning	.29a	.26
Average hours/week planning	.13a	.65
Total hours planning	−.02	.94
Written business plan		.99
Written notes or records		.99
Incorporation	.44	.08
Marketing	−.07	.78
Financial needs & sources	−.10	.70
Balance sheet & income statement	−.06	.82
Facility needs & sources	−.34	.18
Personnel	.06	.81
Organizational design	.47	.06
Client base	−.11	.68
Number of persons sent plan		.99
Capacity of employees at start-up	−.05	.84
Capacity of employees – current or at close	.06	.83
Employees follow standard operating procedure	.61**	.009
Detail of operating procedures	.14	.58
Performance criteria/appraisals used	.38	.13
Single person in command of school	.37	.15
Hours founder/entrepreneur worked first year	−.18	.50
Official recognition by bishop of diocese	−.45	.07
Diocese advertises school	−.46	.06
Only formal communication with diocese	.20	.45
Number of Catholic elementary schools in area	−.07b	.82
Number of Catholic high schools in area	.08c	.78
Stability of the school board	.24	.35

aN = 15. bN = 14. cN = 16.
*p< .05. **p < .01.

As important as it was to perform inferential statistics on the combined sample of schools returning surveys, it was even more important to perform inferential statistics between the open and closed schools to more finely granulize the data (see Table 58). This breakdown revealed additional data between the groups, such as the statistical significance between incorporation and longevity with the open schools (.65) and detailed operating procedures and longevity within the closed schools (.89). A negative correlation became evident in this breakdown in the open school category between "Diocese advertises school" and longevity (-.70) at the < .05 level indicating that there is a statistically negative correlation between the diocese advertising the school and longevity, whereas, there is a significant statistical correlation between (p < .01) the longevity of the open schools (.72) and "only formal communications existing with the diocese." This means that is it highly likely that most open schools have only formal written communications existing with the diocese and diocesan advertising does not affect the longevity of the open schools.

When comparing the one significant correlation of "Employees follow standard operating procedure" from the table of compiled data (see Table 57) to the table showing the breakdown between the open and closed schools (see Table 58), it is interesting to note that while not statistically significant in the table indicating the breakdown between groups, the major difference between the following of operating procedures by the employees and longevity becomes apparent in the closed schools ($r = .74$ and $p = .16$) category in this second table more than the open schools ($r = .23$ and $p = .47$).

Looking at the non-statistically significant variables, the open school group had no additional variables that, according to Fink (2003), had a positive relationship to longevity aside from "A Single Person in Command" at .28 indicating a fair degree of relationship. All other selected variables had little or no positive relationship or a negative relationship on longevity. One would think that the open schools would have more variables correlating to longevity than the closed schools, but this did not seem to be the case. The closed schools had nine additional variables indicating some degree of correlation with longevity with four from the Start-up category: Written Notes or Records, .71; Organizational Design, .58; Number of Weeks Planning, .46; and Total Hours Planning, .41. Three from the Organization category: Employees Follow Standard Operating Procedure, .74; Performance Criteria/Appraisals Used, .67; and Single Person in Command of School, .47. The final two were from the Individual category: Full-Time Experience in Education, .37; and Years Worked in Small Business, .26.

It is interesting to see those variables in the closed group that had a moderate to good relationship according to Fink (2003b). These were: Employees Follow Standard Operating Procedures (.74), Written Notes or Records (.71), Performance Criteria/Appraisals Used (.67), and Organizational Design (.58). Those variables with a fair degree (Fink, 2003b) of correlation to longevity in the closed group were the remaining five of Single Person in Command (.47), Number of Weeks Planning (.46), Total Hours Planning (.41), Full-Time Experience in Education (.37), and Years Worked in Small Business (.26).

Table 58

Spearman Correlations of Selected Questions With Longevity Variable, Open and Closed Schools

Question	Open (N = 12)		Closed (N = 5)	
	r	p	r	p
Full-time experience in education	.07	.83	.37	.54
Years worked in small business	−.25	.44	.26	.67
Prior business start-up	−.39	.21		.99
Highest level of education	.08	.81	.11	.87
Number of weeks planning	-.43	.17	.46	.43
Average hours/week planning	.11a	.75	-.05	.94
Total hours planning	−.30a	.40	.41	.49
Written business plan	.03	.93	-.71	.18
Written notes or records	-.48	.11	.71	.18
Incorporation	.65*	.02	.35	.56
Marketing		.99		.99
Financial needs & sources	.23	.47		
Balance sheet & income statement	−.15	.65	.29	.64
Facility needs & sources	−.16	.63		
Personnel	.23	.47	-.87	.06
Organizational design	.25	.43	.58	.31
Client base	.22	.49	-.87	.06
Number of persons sent plan	-.13	.70	-.45	.45
Capacity of employees at start-up	−.13	.68	-.41	.49
Capacity of employees – current or at close	-.32	.32	-.11	.86
Employees follow standard operating procedure	.23	.47	.74	.16
Detail of operating procedures	-.22	.49	.89*	.04
Performance criteria/appraisals used	.08	.81	.67	.22
Single person in command of school	.28	.38	.47	.42
Hours founder/entrepreneur worked first year	−.46	.13	.10	.87
Official recognition by bishop of diocese	−.57	.06		.99
Diocese advertises school	−.70*	.01		.99
Only formal communication with diocese	.72**	.008	-.71	.18
Number of Catholic elementary schools in area	−.63a	.05	-.80b	.20
Number of Catholic high schools in area	-.44c	.18	-.22	.72
Stability of the school board	.13	.69		

aN = 10. bN = 4. cN = 11.
*p< .05. **p < .01.

Chapter 4: Discussion

Overview of Study

Realizing that 40% of the member schools were no longer in operation, this researcher, who volunteers as an educational consultant and resource coordinator for the NAPC*IS, decided to undertake a study to glean data from current NAPC*IS member schools to determine what components were essential to their start-up and sustainability. Because this is an understudied area and because this researcher consistently received requests for assistance with the start-up of new schools, an observational, explanatory design was used to gather as much data as possible about the founder, the start-up, the organization, and the environment in which these schools operate in order to assist new entrepreneurs in their venture of starting a new school.

Reworking the existing survey of Duchesneau (1987), who incorporated a program-planning model from Van de Ven et al. (1984), this researcher created and tested for validity and reliability, the NSRS. This survey was administered online and through the mail to a target sample of 58 NAPC*IS member schools, consisting of 46 open and 12 closed schools. From the 46 open schools, 12 schools responded to the survey and from the 12 closed schools, 5 responded to the survey. Both descriptive and inferential statistics were performed on the data and results are addressed in the previous chapter. This section will discuss and summarize the results, look at the implications of these findings, and suggest areas for further research.

The Individual

The first question focused on the individual founder or lead entrepreneur of a private, independent Catholic school. In particular, this area addressed the aspects of the individual founder, or entrepreneur's, formal education, small business experience, leadership experience, entrepreneurial experience, personal risk-taking, and personal financial commitment to the school project. This discussion will address the research question, "What are the critical qualities and characteristics of the school founder that lend to a successful start-up and sustainability of an independent Catholic school"?

Formal education. In the open school group, 100% of the founder-entrepreneurs reported having 4 years or more of college, with 2 school founder-entrepreneurs indicating they possess doctoral degrees (see Table 7). The closed schools also had individuals reporting they had at least 1-3 years of college, but no doctoral recipients. The studies cited in the literature review for nascent entrepreneurs (Kim, Aldrick, & Keister 2003; Reynolds & Curtin, 2008) and entrepreneurs in general (Wadhwa et al., 2009) indicated that most entrepreneurs have a minimum of a bachelor's degree with some holding advanced degrees. The results of this study are in line with these previous studies, as well as with Parker and Praag's (2010) study comparing those with more formal education as more likely to initiate new business ventures than to take over existing ones. According to the *National Standards and Benchmarks for effective Catholic Elementary and Secondary Schools* (Ozar et al., 2012), administrators of Catholic schools should meet national, state, or (Arch) diocesan requirements and obtain licensure. In the state of Florida, this would be a master's degree. With this qualification 41.7% of the open school founders and 60% of the closed school founders would not qualify for administration in Catholic schools because they do not hold a master's degree or above. Fifty-eight percent of the open school founders would qualify under this category. Forty-one percent of those administrators currently operating successful NAPC*IS schools would be eliminated under these particular benchmarks. The inferential statistics of both the open and closed groups indicated no statistical significance between the highest level of education and longevity (see Table 57). There must be something in addition to a master's degree and licensure that keeps these successful schools operating; perhaps it is the combination of education and experience that assists with successful operation. NAPC*IS, as well as ACCS, require that the school leader have the "education and experience appropriate to the positions" and meet the school's written requirements for the position they hold. These requirements are left to the individual schools in the ACCS membership. According to these requirements, both open and closed school founders would qualify if they met the school's requirements. Of course these requirements could be more restrictive or more liberal.

The data indicate that more formally educated individuals (4 years or more of college) are willing to undertake a new educational venture than individuals who have not had a minimum of 4 years of college. The formal education of the founder would be important for potential stakeholders to know, but whether or not the founder-entrepreneur possesses a master's degree would not be an overriding component because 41.7% of successful private NAPC*IS schools are currently led by individuals with only 4-year college degrees. The inferential statistics for the closed schools in Table 58 indicate a fair degree of relationship between full time experience in education and longevity indicating that a combination of components assists in the longevity of the schools.

Small business. Both the open (83.34%) and closed (80%) school founder-entrepreneurs self-reported to have worked previously between 1 and "over 16 years" in small businesses (see Table 3). Wagner's (2004) study found a statistical significance of new start-ups coming from individuals who were previously employed in young or small firms. The data in the study also indicates that founders of NAPC*IS schools have small business experience. In the combined report (Table 57), this small business experience is not statistically significant to longevity, but when broken out between the open and closed schools (Table 58), the closed schools indicate a fair degree of relationship (.26) (Fink, 2003) between small business experience and longevity. Again, because some of the closed schools who responded were open past the average closure rate of 6.14 years, small business experience cannot be discounted.

When comparing NAPC*IS founder-entrepreneurs to Catholic school principals in the category of previous small business experience, the NAPC*IS school founders clearly have more previous business experience (80-83.34%) than the Catholic school principals (Diamond, 1987). Diamond (1987) reported that only one-third of the principals had previous professional experience. As self-reported by principals in Schuttloffel's (2003) study, 32% stated one of their highest deficit areas was the lack of administrative skills. These types of skills are generally found in a business setting.

With previous small business skills, NAPC*IS founders-entrepreneurs have one factor of a skill-set that Catholic school principals wish they possessed. These administrative skills can include many different areas, from customer service to filing, accounting to management. Having previous exposure to learn these skills and improve them over time allows the administrator to focus on more areas of expertise such as curriculum development, personnel issues, or faith formation.

Previous leadership experience. Fifty-eight percent of the open school founders had previous supervisory experience supervising between 3-250 employees. Thirty-three percent supervised between 51-250 employees and 41.7% supervised between 0-2 employees. Forty percent of the closed school founder-entrepreneurs had minimal supervisory experience, supervising only 0-2 employees. Schuttloffel (2003) noted that 51% of newly hired principals had 0-3 years of school leadership experience and that most of them had "recently left the classroom" (p. 13). These newly hired Catholic school principals would equate to the 40% of founder-entrepreneurs from either the closed or open schools, so in this regard they are comparable (see Table 4), but at 58%, NAPC*IS open school founder-entrepreneurs have previously supervised more employees than newly hired Catholic school principals.

Previous start-up experience. The findings from this survey in regard to previous start-up experience are in line with Reynolds and Curtin's (2008) report on the PSED and PSEDII study on entrepreneurs. Reynolds and Curtin reported that 54% (PSED) and 62% (PSEDII) of men and women did not possess previous start-up business experience and that an average of 20% of men and women in both studies had only one previous start-up venture. The combined percentages, per study, of 74% (PSED) and 82% (PSEDII) are similar to the results of this survey for both open and closed schools. Ninety-one percent of open schools and 100% of closed schools had entrepreneurs with little previous start-up experience. Unlike the PSED and PSEDII studies that found 25% of men and women surveyed had experience with five or more start-up businesses, only 8.3%, or one individual, from the NAPC*IS open school category reported to have opened seven or more businesses.

A correlation did not exist between previous start-up experience and longevity (see Table 57 and Table 58). What previous start-ups may have done was to help the founder with the "intrapreneurial" thinking that goes along with starting a new business venture (Kessler & Frank, 2009). Individuals with previous entrepreneurial experience would perhaps be more likely and willing to do another start-up since they had been through it once before. Knowing that an individual had previous start-up experience, whether with another school, or a business, helps with the transfer of "intrapreneurial" concepts applicable to a new school venture.

Personal risk taking. When looking at the sense of risk-taking on the part of the founder-entrepreneur, it is valuable to look at the other correlations of 'outside funding at start-up' and 'personal investment in the school' (see Table 55 and Table 56). According to Fink (2003), there is a fair degree of relationship at start-up in the combined group of open and closed schools (.37), but when broken down between the open and closed schools, it is the closed schools that report a fair degree (Fink, 2003) of correlation between personal risk and outside funding (see Table 56). Seventy-five percent of the open school founder-entrepreneurs perceived small to no risk if the school failed (see Table 6) compared to 40% of the closed schools. Ninety-one percent of the open schools received between only $0-50,000 upon opening and one founder reported receiving $200,001 and above (see Table 9). Sixty percent of the closed school founders perceived their risk to be either "some" or "great," yet they also reported unanimously that they received between $0-50,000 upon opening. Clearly, there was more of a sense of risk on the part of the closed school founders-entrepreneurs than open school founders, perhaps because they had more of a personal financial investment in the school (see Table 7 and Personal Financial Commitment below). These mixed findings regarding risk-taking mirror the research in the literature review. Brockhaus (1980) and Miner and Raju (2004) found that risk-taking was not a determining characteristic of entrepreneurs and that entrepreneurs were more risk-avoidant. Conversely, Pines et al. (2012) found a significant correlation between risk-taking propensity and entrepreneurial traits and Fernald, Solomon, & Tarabishy (2005) found in a review of 136 research-based studies and peer-reviewed articles that risk-taking was one of the most mentioned characteristics.

Founders or entrepreneurs in closed schools reported a sense of risk from small to great at 80% and founders-entrepreneurs of open schools reported 58.3% at the same levels. Again, the closed school founders-entrepreneurs perceived a greater sense of risk at the beginning of their undertaking than did the leaders of the open NAPC*IS schools. According to Fink (2003) there is a fair degree of correlation between personal risk and outside funding for closed schools at start-up of .47. This is confirmed by the descriptive and inferential statistics (see Tables 6 and 56). Conversely, open school founders perceived small to no risk (Table 6) and little to no correlation (Fink, 2003) exists between their perceived personal risk and outside funding at start-up and their personal risk and outside funding currently.

Personal financial commitment. Eighty percent of closed NAPC*IS school founders had anywhere from $1,001–40,000 of personal funds invested in the new school start-up compared to 50% of the open NAPC*IS school founders. The open NAPC*IS schools had two founders or 16.7%, reporting they had $60,001 and above invested in the new start-up. Open school founders also reported that 50% of them had only $0-1,000 invested in the new start-up as compared to one or 20% of the closed school founders. While 80% of the closed schools had committed a substantial amount of money toward the start-up, in total their funds could be no more than $100,000, whereas the total funding possible for the open schools is $92,002 and above. Because the bracket that was chosen by the open school founders of "$60,001 and above" does not have an upper limit, the amount that was invested is unknown, but could extend beyond the $100,000 mark of the closed schools. The open schools had more schools with less invested by their founders at start-up (50% at $0-1,000) (see Table 7).

This low investment amount on the part of open NAPC*IS schools mirrors the report of Kim et al. (2003) who noted that 50% of new ventures required only $2,000, and 80% of the new ventures started with under $10,000, in line with the NAPC*IS minimal recommendation of $250 personal commitment (E. Cubanski, personal communication, January 9, 2013). It seems that a founder does not really need "lots of capital" for an initial start-up and that less than $1,000 has been sufficient for NAPC*IS schools. When reviewing the inferential statistics to see if any correlation existed between personal investment of the founder at start-up and outside funding received at start-up no correlation existed within the open schools (see Table 56), and only a fair degree of correlation (.48) existed in the closed schools. As founders of closed schools contributed to start-up expenses so did outside sources. No direct correlation existed within the open schools where open school founders contributed significantly less toward start-up costs than closed school founders, yet each group received almost the same in outside resources (see Table 9).

Full-time experience in the field of education. Forty-one percent of the open school founders report having had between 6-16 or more years in the field of education prior to opening their school (see Table 2). Thirty-three percent of these founders had between 1-5 years in education. Experienced school founders with between 1–16 or more years of full-time education experience were attributed to 75% of open schools with 25% never having had full-time education experience. The closed schools reported 80% of their founders with between 1-10 years of full-time education experience. No founders from the closed schools had more than 10 years of full-time education experience.

It is difficult to compare the results from this study to the results from Schuttloffel's (2003) study of Catholic school principals as reported by their superintendents because the ranges of experience are not the same. NAPC*IS open school administrators had previous full-time experience at 0 - 5 years at 58% and in Schuttloffel's (2003) study a similar group (0 – 3 years) had previous experience in the field of education at 51%. In both studies, however, newer and less experienced administrators of schools were the majority.

Conclusions and summaries for the individual. To characterize a founder-entrepreneur of successful NAPC*IS schools, one would find someone with between 0 – 5 years of full-time experience in the field of education, more previous supervisory experience, someone with a minimum of 4 years or more of college and who has small to no personal risk involved in the new start-up. This individual may or may not have previous start-up experience. A total of 41.7% of the administrators of open, successful schools (as defined in this survey), do not have a master's degree, which is contrary to the requirements for administrators established by the National Standards and Benchmarks for effective Catholic Elementary and Secondary Schools (Ozar et al., 2012), yet they are operating "successful" schools as measured by this study. From this researcher's personal experience, founders of NAPC*IS schools are not interested in obtaining licensures from national or state agencies; this is contrary to one of the many reasons they are opening up a private independent school. They seek the freedom to choose their own curriculum and teachers, to make improvements, and to perform annual evaluations according to the standards they feel are in line with the mission of their school, not according to outside agencies.

Implications. This information can help guide a search committee that is seeking to hire a school administrator for a private, independent Catholic school or a philanthropist or banker who is considering financing a new venture. Based on the fact that 41.7% of the successful open school founders or lead administrators had only four years of college, search teams should not discount individuals applying for this position and who do not have a Master's degree or above, but who have significant previous supervisory experience. Open school founders reported having more previous supervisory experience with 33.3% reporting to have 11 or more years of full-time work in the field of education compared to 0% of the school founders or lead administrators in closed schools (see Table 2). These individuals all reported below 10 years of previous experience in the field of education. Searching for someone who has supervised more employees would be comparable to the open school founders who reported having more experience supervising between 11-250 employees at a time compared to the closed school founders who only supervised between 11-50 employees and none higher (see Table 3). This study also indicated that searching for someone with previous start-up experience was not necessary for a successful school since the majority of both open (91.7%) and closed (100%) school founders or lead administrators reported similar previous start-up experience (see Table 6).

NAPC*IS advised that the initial administrator of the school be a member of the board of trustees or the actual founder. The definition for founder used in the research survey is broader than the meaning attached by NAPC*IS (2013d) and includes an individual who was an early employee, or in this case, the first head of school or principal. This person is not necessarily a member of the incorporating board. Selection of a board member to fulfill the requirements of the NAPC*IS feasibility guidelines as the initial head of school may result in the scenario we are seeing within the closed schools and described under The Organization – Leadership Style in this chapter. Significant involvement by the Board in the day-to-day administration of the school and a founder-entrepreneur who governs the Board and acts in the capacity of the Head of School provides little distance to distribute and delegate decision making and little opportunity for buy-in of additional stakeholders (parents and teachers) into the school. In addition to the actual successful school founder-entrepreneur characterized above (see Conclusions and summaries for the individual) it seems that someone who fits the characteristics of the successful school founder-entrepreneur, who can refrain from board involvement in the day-to-day operations of the school, can also be considered as a candidate for the Head of School.

The Start-Up Procedures

Question 2 addressed start-up procedures used by founders or lead entrepreneurs to plan, market, and open their schools. Specific areas addressed in this section included whether a market analysis was performed or potential families queried about the proposed new project, were other alternatives and options for schooling sought, how much time was spent on planning for the new school, were potential families and other professionals involved in the start-up, and whether or not a formal business plan or written notes and records were used to aid start-up. This discussion answers the research question, "What are the critical issues and components that must be addressed in the start-up process of opening an independent Catholic school"?

When looking at the results from the three questions that addressed the program planning model used in the framework study (Van de Ven & Koening, 1976) of market analysis-potential families contacted (see Appendix B, 1.201a) alternative ways and means (see Appendix B, 1.201b), and professional involvement in developing the business plan (see Appendix B, 1.204, 1.204a-d), it was interesting to note that both open and closed schools reported to have performed these steps at least to some degree. In the open school group only one school reported not to have involved professionals in the development of the business plan (see Table 15) and four schools, or 33%, of open schools did not seek alternative ways and means to solve their issue of schooling for their children (see Table 11). It seems that once the decision was made to open a school, little or no other educational alternatives were sought, and founders moved immediately forward seeking professional assistance, performing market analyses, and contacting potential families. The program planning model advocates for a needs analysis, data collection, and cross-generational and professional input into the project and states that entrepreneurial efforts that incorporate at least some aspects of the program planning model have more successful start-ups (Van de Ven & Koenig, 1976). Even though it appears the efforts on behalf of both groups to almost completely eliminate the search for alternative educational choices, they did incorporate the first three phases of the Program

Planning Model to some degree, and all were successful in opening their schools.

Whether to spend a considerable amount of time planning for a new venture or to work and make adjustments "on-the-fly" has been an area of current entrepreneurial research (Brinckman, Grichnik, & Kapsa, 2010; Castrogiovanni, 1996). Pre-planning is advocated from the results of most research (Brinckmann et al., 2010; Gruber, 2007; Kessler & Frank, 2009), but the writing of a formal business plan was not warranted unless the entrepreneur was seeking venture capital (Lange, Mollov, Pearlmutter, Singh, & Bygrave, 2007). The majority of both the open (91.7%) and closed (80%) schools used written notes instead of a formal business plan (see Table 20), and while not statistically significant the use of written notes had a moderate to good correlation to longevity within the closed schools (see Table 58).

A major company assisting diocesan Catholic schools and parishes with strategic planning is the Meitler (2012) group. Their strategic planning process mirrors the process by Van de Ven and Koenig (1976) and includes working with the diocesan hierarchy for approval of the new project. NAPC*IS schools are independent, private entities whose authority for operating comes from the state where they are located. They are required to be incorporated for state approval. Incorporation was one variable that was statistically significant for longevity in open schools (.65) and identified as having a fair relationship (.35) to longevity in closed schools (see Table 58). The correlation between incorporation and longevity in both groups is not surprising.

Phase four of the Program Planning Model (Van de Ven & Koenig, 1976) involved identifying local leaders to implement the plan. This included the hiring of individuals to operate the school and make up the initial administrative team and organizational hierarchy. Results for both the open and closed schools indicated organizational design at start-up as having a fair degree of relationship to longevity at .47 (see Table 57). When breaking out the two groups, this was also evident in the closed schools at .58 (see Table 58). It had little to no relationship in the open school group.

Question 1.202 (see Appendix B) pertained to the number of total hours and weeks a founder or entrepreneur put into the planning of the new school. While not addressing a specific amount of time, Brinckmann et al. (2010) reported that entrepreneurs and small business owners who were faithful to the process of planning, as well as the culminating plans, had increased firm performance. They emphasized flexibility and that planning and execution should be carried out simultaneously and that "long pre-planning activities detached from market interaction and feedback appear(ed) detrimental" (p. 15). When looking at the results from Table 14, one can see that the closed schools averaged 6 more weeks of planning than the open schools, but their total number of planning hours is less than open schools. From Table 58 the closed schools showed a fair correlation to longevity in the Total Hours Planning whereas the open schools showed a negative correlation to longevity. Both the open and closed schools indicated they took the time for planning their new venture and both groups were successful at starting their operations. This is in line with the research of Brinckman et al. (2010) and Kessler and Frank (2009), that some type of pre-planning is beneficial for a successful start-up. But how much planning time is enough planning time? Reynolds and Curtain's (2008) report from the PSED II indicated that most new firms take an average of 2 years before start-up and, on average, 5 years before these firms become successful. The PSEDII results (Reynolds & Curtain, 2008) reported that an average start-up team consisting of 1.7 members averaged 1,500 total hours of pre-planning prior to the commencement of business. This equates to 22 weeks of work at 40 hours per week per person. This is under the average number of weeks reported by both the open and closed schools (see Table 14). The Program Planning Model of Van de Ven and Koenig (1976), as well as the Meitler (2012) planning process, both heavily emphasized a systematic approach to new venture start-up with three to seven phases and an extensive pre-planning timeframe, while Gruber's (2007) study indicated that the amount of planning should be dependent upon the dynamics of the environment and the necessity of speed in decision making. The opening up of a new school likely would need to take into account the annual enrollment cycles of the local school systems (both public and private). Planning for the new school venture could be expedited to current or future cycles dependent upon other required variables. It would seem from the reported number of weeks spent in planning (see Table 14) for both the open (28 weeks) and closed schools (34 weeks), that these groups expedited their planning process to under one year, perhaps to target the new enrollment cycle. This would be in keeping with the adaptive business planning model based upon the dynamics of the environment as described by Gruber (2007) in his research on 100 start-up businesses. When looking at the correlation between the numbers of weeks spent in planning (.29) and longevity for the combined group of schools (see Table 57), there is only a fair degree of relationship to longevity. There is little relationship between the number of hours per week spent planning (.13) or total hours spent planning (-.02) and longevity.

While the request for starting a new diocesan school must go through the local bishop, superintendent and other advisory committees (Kealey, 1997), NAPC*IS schools must only seek approval for setting up operations from state and local civil agencies. They are not required to seek approval for operating as an educational institution from a local Catholic bishop. The diocesan process included also receiving the approval of the surrounding pastors whose parishes are adjacent to the potential new school. Budgets and construction costs were then prepared. Seventy-five percent of the open schools and 90% of the closed schools did not use an architect at start-up (see Table 19). Only 41.7% of the open schools indicated they prepared professional financial statements (e.g., balance sheet and income statements) (see Table 12). What NAPC*IS schools seemed to rely upon were notes that detailed financial needs and resources as well as facility needs and resources (see Table 12). Generally, an accountant, or someone with accounting experience would prepare financial statements, and, quite possibly, a formal business plan. Seventy-five percent of the open schools and 80% of the closed schools indicated they did not use an accountant. This is quite unlike the diocesan process, yet the majority (58.3%) of open schools that did not prepare these formal financial statements (see Table 12) or use an accountant (75%; see Table 17) are considered successful in this research because they are still open and operating. What these schools did use was an attorney. Generally an attorney would assist someone with the incorporation process. This seemed to be the case for the open (67.3%) schools, but not the closed (40%) schools (see Table 16). The diocesan procedure did include the use of an attorney to assist with land purchases. Incorporation of a diocesan school would not be necessary, but paperwork detailing any loans, construction, encumbrances upon the diocese or local parish, and other legal areas would be handled by the diocesan attorney.

The next step in starting a diocesan school, fundraising, was not indicated as having as high a priority at start-up in the open NAPC*IS schools group (41.7%) as in the closed school group (60.0%). In the Order of Start-up Procedures (see Figure 1) for

ACCS schools, fundraising ranked 14 out of 21. It is ranked 27th, or last, for NAPC*IS schools, but holds a pronounced place in the diocesan planning process. While part of the opening procedures for both NAPC*IS and the ACCS, it is not mentioned in the Program Planning Model, since this model has basically been used by for-profit businesses, and the decision as to whether the new venture would be financially feasible is determined early on in the planning process. The opening of a private, independent Catholic school, as well as the Christian ACCS schools, has more to do with the spiritual call to the apostolate of education than a desire for financial gain. Many of the NAPC*IS schools started with very little outside funding. Only one NAPC*IS open school reported any significant outside funding prior to opening (see Table 9). Each school then had to create budgets for sustainability and, as this researcher has witnessed and experienced, many had to include fund-raising as a significant part of the operating budget.

Conclusion and summary. There are many interdependent variables that go into the start-up of a new school. Some of these variables play a more prominent role than others, such as using written notes instead of creating a formal business plan, incorporation, a planning process and consideration to the initial organizational design. Reynolds (2011) stated that no one specific factor alone will make or break the start-up process. Gruber (2007) advocated for an adaptive start-up process and this is what all the NAPC*IS schools (both open and closed) have done. Almost the full majority of both open and closed schools have opened without significant outside funding and some contact with potential families. It seems once these schools decided to open they sought few alternatives and moved forward investing anywhere from 28-34 hours toward the project during the workweek in a span of time that amounted to less than one school year.

Implications. Individuals who are interested in opening a private, independent Catholic school should include some sort of planning process in their start-up phase, but need not spend financial resources on the preparation of formal financial statements when written notes and reports have proven helpful for the majority of both open and closed schools. While the reporting schools have limited their planning timeframe to less than one year, research indicates that a systematic planning process, and the outcomes from that process, should be adaptive to the business environment (Gruber, 2007). Individuals interested in opening a school should consider the use of an attorney to prepare the incorporation papers and initial formation documents and expect to open up with less than $50,000 received from outside sources.

The Organization

Question 3 was quite broad and included the areas of the capacity of the personnel of the school at a specific times, to what degree founders used distributed leadership by measuring shared decision making throughout the school, the standardization and detail of performance evaluations and operating systems, time and effort of the founder, and the utilization ratio of current students to possible students. This discussion addresses the research question, "What are the essential early organizational decisions and strategies that will aid in the success of a new private independent Catholic school?"

Capacity. A review of the literature indicated mixed research regarding the capacity of individual employees at start-up (Duchesneau, 1987; Frederickson & Mitchell, 1984; March & Simon, 1958). The framework study by Duchesneau (1987) indicated that high levels of specialization of workers led to unsuccessful start-ups.

Boone and Hendricks (2009) stated that this diversity (in the sense of a cross-function of content knowledge) within top management teams was beneficial as long as the individuals worked in a collaborative manner, shared accurate information, and had a decentralized decision-making process. The question used in this research study focused on the capacity of the individual employees at start-up and again at either the closing of the school or when the survey was completed. The results in this research study indicated that both open (66.7%) and closed (60%) NAPC*IS schools had individuals who were more specialized in their abilities at the start-up of the school (see Table 23). This contradicts the framework study, but because of the narrow scope of the question, it does not accurately indicate whether the specialization of the group of individuals contributed positively or negatively to a diverse management team as researched in the Boone and Hendricks (2009) study.

It was interesting to note that the capacity of the individuals in the open schools expanded at the time the survey was completed moving from 33.3% to 75% (see Table 23 and Table 24). This is in line with the public and Catholic school literature of Stewart (2013) and Bolotta (2012) that indicated the need to raise student achievement through capacity building of school personnel and even those in the surrounding community who could support the school and its students.

Both the open and closed schools seemed to follow the advice from the *NAPC*IS Feasibility Packet* (NAPC*IS, 2013b) that states to focus on hiring well-formed Catholic school graduates instead of more experienced educators, Catholic or non-Catholic. The open NAPC*IS schools built the capacity of their employees by 41.7%, whereas the closed school capacity did not change from opening to closing. This capacity building could have been accomplished in many ways, such as professional development for current teachers, administrators, and support staff (para-professionals), or by hiring individuals with multiple areas of expertise.

Leadership styles. Questions 1.305 through 1.307 (see Appendix B) addressed the degree to which those running the school practiced distributed leadership by measuring to what extent decision making was diffused throughout personnel associated with the school. Clawson (2012) stated that effective organizations are built around information systems that empower companies to use "flatter" organizational styles where those directly involved with the issue are empowered to make decisions with the vision, mission, and goals of the corporation in mind. This flatter organizational model lends itself to distributed leadership, where working in teams, using collaborative skills for shared decision making and responsibility, is becoming more evident in schools (Leithwood, Day, Sammons, Harris, & Hopkins, 2007). Leithwood et al. (2009) also reported on distributed leadership in schools and stated that the way leadership was distributed was more important than the distribution itself. They noted that purposeful and planned leadership distributed throughout the school, positively impacted school development, change, and student outcomes.

When looking at the closed schools in this research, it became evident that they seemed to be operating with a leadership that was very close-knit, especially when looking at the percentage that the board was active in the daily work activities of the school (40% for closed and 25% for open) (see Table 32). Questions 1.305 asked to what degree a single person was in charge of the school (see Appendix B). The closed schools had 60% reporting that a single person was in charge "to a substantial extent" or "to a great extent." This left 40% reporting "to a small extent." If a single person was not in charge then who was in charge? By default this would mean that numerous individuals shared "command" of the school. Question 1.307a (see Appendix B) asked to what extent board members were involved in making decisions on how work activities are performed in the schools. This is generally left to the discretion of the head of school or principal. Board members in closed schools were more involved in making decisions about these daily work activities (40% for "quite a bit" and "very much") than board members of open schools (25%, "quite a bit"). Teachers in closed schools were also not allowed to have as much to say about setting goals and strategies (see Table 31), and even administrators in closed schools had less to say in this area (see Table 30). It would be fair to say that the board had a substantial involvement in the daily operations of the school and that very few distributed leadership characteristics were evident. When correlating the variable regarding a single person in charge of the school with longevity in the closed school category (see Table 58), the Spearman Rho correlation was .47 indicating a fair degree of relationship between command and longevity, but it was not a statistically significant relationship. Depending upon the size and expertise of the board members, the one characteristic of being a "flatter" organization, with the ability of board members to make quicker, long-lasting and foundational decisions on-the-spot seems to be a positive according to Clawson (2012). But the inability to decentralize control and to provide a cushion between daily operations and board responsibilities may have acted as a hindrance to overall school success. This is in line with Guernsey and Barott's (2008) initial study on conflict within independent Catholic schools and the characteristic of the founders of these start-up schools to heavily protect the school's existence by "maintaining unilateral control of all aspects of the school" and to "seal off managerial-level power" (p. 491). By heavily protecting their existence (their mission, curriculum, philosophy of education, and so forth), these schools screened many potential families who they deemed not in line with this mission, and, therefore, not a fit for the school. By being highly selective, they threatened their financial viability, since these schools operate primarily on tuition dollars. Also, with such direct supervision by the board over daily operations of the school, the founders hoped to "seal off power from other stakeholders" who might desire to gain control of the school through social influence. Guernsey and Barott (1983) cited Iannaccone's (1983) observation stating that

> Once a person or group possesses an established power, the individual or group is often so concerned with protecting the rights and privileges such power brings, and clings to power so blindly, that they risk destroying the very entity or organization upon which their power is based. (Iannaccone, p. 495)

The small schools that operate with such oppressive board influence become extensions of those who found them. They are what Guernsey and Barott (1983) call "personal" schools instead of "private" schools and while established in this way, some private, independent Catholic schools have been able to institutionalize their schools, creating that cushion or separation between the oversight of the board and the daily decision making of the principal, or head of school, that is so important to absorb areas of conflict and descent and allow for the opportunities of democratic change without the departure of unsatisfied families or personnel. The question is, when, and how, does a founder move from the personal call of the apostolate to education, or the pure human desire for independence, to institutionalizing the new venture? The question is partially answered by looking at the results of the open school responses in this section.

Open NAPC*IS schools can be characterized as managed in a more traditional, business-like approach, with a single individual in charge of the school (91.7% combined "substantial" to "great extent," see Table 27) and with teachers who have more of a say in setting goals and developing strategies (58.3% "quite a bit," see Table 31). Administrators in open schools are included at a higher percentage in making decisions on goals and strategies (91.6% combined "quite a bit" and "very much," see Table 29) and daily work activities (91.7% combined "quite a bit" and "very much," see Table 32), and there was a reduction of board member involvement in the daily decision making on work activities (25% combined "quite a bit" and "very much," see Table 31). These percentages indicate a higher degree of involvement, and more involvement, of various individuals connected with the school. Coupling this with the capacity building of personnel as noted above, one can see the increase in stakeholder involvement in the operations of open schools, quite unlike that of the closed schools. Interestingly, open schools, as previously reported in this chapter under Start-up, spent more time on Organizational Design (see Table 12) which includes identifying required personnel, writing job descriptions, delineating reporting procedures, and so forth, than closed schools. This pre-planning of organizational design work can help facilitate an organizational structure that is more institutionalized where more distributed types of leadership approaches are possible.

As mentioned in the literature review, leadership style and leadership theory in public schools have mirrored that of businesses. Catholic schools have also followed the trends and have incorporated these styles into their faith-based operations adding a unique derivative from transformational leadership called "servant" leadership. School leaders exemplifying servant leadership may inspire others to serve through their own personal example and delegate to others the "opportunities to share the mantle of leadership" (Bolotta, 2013, p. 9). By working as a broad-based team of individuals with a stake in the development of goals and strategies, more individuals are given the opportunity to serve in more unified and combined ways. Whether servant leadership was exhibited by the founder or head of school is not known from the data gathered in this survey, but the fact that delegation of decision making was reported to increase the probability that some of the characteristics of transformational leadership (where collaboration and delegation are key characteristics) allows the opportunity of servant leadership to be present. Belmonte and Cranston (2009) reported that this collaborative approach to leadership might not work within a traditionally male, autocratic and hierarchical structure of the Catholic Church. NAPC*IS schools do not operate within this spectrum. An autocratic approach to leadership on the part of female principals within Catholic schools has been reported in the literature (Yeager, Benson, Guerra, & Manno, 1985) though, but recent literature regarding Catholic school leaders has focused on the need for these individuals to understand accounting, business, personnel (Ozar, 2010), marketing, social media, the worth of a value-laden curriculum (Cimino, 2010), enrollment management, financial management, development, and marketing (Nuzzi, Holter, & Frabutt, 2013). For survey brevity, all of these particular areas were not queried when looking at the leadership style of the NAPC*IS founder or head of school. These areas would make excellent fodder for further study on the founders and heads of school in NAPC*IS schools.

The one guideline that NAPC*IS has regarding a leader's approach within a school is that leaders should always remember their position is not about power or control, but about responsibility (NAPC*IS, 2013d). When reviewing Guernsey and Barott's (2008) work on conflict within independent schools and how this leads to the split and opening up of new schools, one can see that power and ego are very much a part of these schools, and perhaps their very viability. By the direct involvement of board members in the daily operations of the school and the reduction of involvement of the rank-and-file school community, the issue of power and control are quite evident and should be reflected upon in light of sustainability and viability of the school.

Standardization and detail: Performance evaluations. The use of performance evaluations have helped to objectify the work of employees and have helped to better identify areas for employee improvement and retention opportunities. Like management and leadership theory, these evaluations have evolved over time and made their way from business into public and private schools. Today, performance evaluations are more stressful for public school teachers because in some instances they are tied to student achievement reports, considered as value-added data, as well as instructional and administrative performance (David, 2010). This evaluation has a direct relationship to teacher retention and has become highly controversial (Marshall, 2012). Aside from the value-added performance evaluations, others have stressed the importance of performance evaluations in the school environment (Kane & Cantrell, 2012; Varlas, 2012; Williams, McKinney, Garland, & Goodwin, 2010).

Gaudio's (2008) research revealed very little information regarding performance evaluations in Catholic schools from the NCEA. One needs to review the information from individual dioceses across the country to glean data regarding the use and method for these procedures. Through this exercise, it was revealed that dioceses, for the most part, used a formative evaluation method with the objective of improving student outcomes and did not rely on value-added data such as parent-teacher surveys, portfolios, or student achievement scores.

NAPC*IS provides little guidance regarding performance evaluations aside from several teacher and principal checklists on its website stating that these evaluations should be performed by the head of school and may include both formal and informal observations. Both responding open and closed NAPC*IS schools reported the use of performance procedures for evaluation with the open schools using these procedures 35% more than the closed schools. Closed NAPC*IS schools used performance evaluations "not at all" or "to a small extent" at 60%, whereas open NAPC*IS schools emphasized the use of these evaluations "to a substantial extent" or "to a great extent" at 75%. This data gives additional weight to the perspective that the open schools have become more institutionalized than the closed schools were. Interestingly, the Spearman Rho correlation of the use of performance procedures for evaluation and longevity was not statistically significant at .38 (see Table 57) for the combined groups. When breaking the combined group out into the open and closed schools, the closed schools had a much higher correlation rate ($r = .67$) than the open schools ($r = .08$). According to Fink (2003b), a .67 indicates a moderate to good correlation, but even this was not statistically significant.

Standardization and detail: Operating systems. Whether the reporting schools used standardized procedures for student learning (Goodwin, 2013) or administrative efforts (Bellamy, Crawford, Marshall, & Coulter, 2005) was not detailed in this survey; only the acknowledgment that some type of standard operating procedure as determined by the individual completing the survey (i.e., the founder, head of school, entrepreneur, etc.) as being in place and the extent and detail in which this standardized procedures were used. Having procedures in place for anything from fire and tornado drills to identifying areas of student weakness enhance the capacity of the school and allow personnel to respond in a quicker and more efficient way. Both open and closed NAPC*IS schools reported that their employees followed standard operating procedures and policies "to some extent" or "to a great extent" at 100%. The open schools reported that employees follow these procedures "to a great extent" at 66.7%, whereas the closed school employees followed these procedures "to a great extent" at 20%. This was the only variable correlating with longevity that was statistically significant at .61 ($p < .01$) on the Spearman Rho correlation for the combined group (see Table 57). When breaking the combined group into the open and closed school categories, the correlation between employees follow standard operating procedure and longevity for the closed school was .74 (see Table 58). While not statistically significant, it still has a correlation to longevity. What was statistically significant for the closed schools was the detail of the operating procedures and the longevity of the school at .89 ($p < .05$). It is interesting to see such high correlations within the closed school category for employees following standard operating procedure and the detail of these procedures. Again, it may be that the active presence of the board in closed schools lends to a more controlling and detailed environment. Other than the variable of the use of written notes and records at start-up (see discussion in Start-up above), these three variables within the closed school category had the highest correlation to longevity, yet employees in open schools followed more specific operating procedures and were evaluated to a greater extent in open schools. Clearly, some type of performance evaluations and standardized operating procedures are important for the success of NAPC*IS schools.

Time and effort. Current research is more detailed as to the stages of start-up of new business ventures than the framework study used in this research by Duchesneau (1987) and his predecessor Van de Ven et al. (1984). In keeping with the use of the framework study, Question 1.308a asked how many total hours the lead entrepreneur (founder) worked during the first year following the opening of the school. This was considered within the start-up phase for Duchesneau and Van de Ven, but not so with contemporary entrepreneurial researchers. Kessler and Frank (2009) considered one year after opening a successive phase of a new business. Kessler and Frank's start-up began with the entrepreneur vocalizing his or her intention to open a business and continued until the time the business actually opened its doors. This would be when it would fall out of their start-up category having succeeded in its efforts.

Duchesneau (1987) reported that lead entrepreneurs spent an average of 65 hours per week on the job the first year of start-up. Open NAPC*IS schools reported that 66.7% of lead entrepreneurs or founders spent over 50 hours plus per week during the first year after opening with 33.3% reporting to spend over 60 hours per week but under 70 hours per week on the job. Thirty-three percent of open school entrepreneurs or founders spent forty hours or less per week on the job during the first year of operations. The closed NAPC*IS school entrepreneurs or founders ranged equally from 40 hours per week or less to over 70 hours per week. Sixty percent spent over 50 hours or more per week on the new school effort. It would seem that both groups of school founders spent almost an equivalent amount of time during the first year working at the school, but that more open school founders spent over the average reported by Duchesneau of 63 hours per week with 50% reporting to have spent over 60 hours per week during the first year of the school. It would not be surprising that school founders would report more time on the job than industry leaders. The head administrative position within a school has been noted for its importance and sometimes overwhelming time requirements (Dygert, 2000), and in the desire to not only fulfill these requirements, but to start up a new operation, these individuals would need to devote considerably more time to the overall start-up effort.

Utilization ratio. O'Meara et al.'s (2012) research indicated that the actual enrollment as compared to the potential enrollment of 400 Catholic elementary schools in the United States had a high correlation (.895) to the financial stability of the school, thus in turn lending the school toward financial stability and viability. Two questions were created to glean data from NAPC*IS schools to see if there was any comparison between these Catholic schools and the private independent schools. Indeed there was. The open schools' ratio of current students to maximal capacity of students was 72.5% compared to the report from the closed schools of only 43.6% (see Table 44). A direct causation between the servicing ratios of current to maximum students and school closings cannot be made, but from the data gleaned in this survey, it would be something to be watched. More importantly, the additional correlations identified by O'Meara et al. (2012) would also be worth reviewing, especially square footage to total revenue, and salaries to total revenue, expense, and tuition.

Conclusion and summary. Both open and closed NAPC*IS schools indicated that individual employees at start-up were more specialized indicating a narrowed capacity at start-up. This specialization of individuals could have been beneficial to the mix of personnel as a group, if collaboration and decision making based on accurate information existed. The capacity of personnel expanded by 41.7% from start-up to the completing of the survey by the open school founder. Open schools had more personnel involved in goal setting and strategy development as well as the daily work activities of the school. Closed schools indicated more board involvement in daily operations. Open NAPC*IS schools used employee evaluations and standard operating procedures, but were not as detail oriented as closed NAPC*IS schools. Both the open and closed school founders spent a significant amount of time at the school each averaging well over 50 hours per week on the new venture. Open schools had a higher ratio of students served to the number of potential students the school could serve.

Implications. Leaders of existing NAPC*IS schools should find ways to increase the capacity of their personnel through workshops, off- or on-site coursework, and programs or other types of professional development. Not only has research indicated that this has an effect on student outcomes, but it does mirror the practice of the successful open NAPC*IS schools. When considering organizational design, NAPC*IS school entrepreneurs should make special consideration to the distinction between "flatter" organizations where more immediate decisions can be make more quickly at lower levels of subsidiarity, and the fact that having separate layers within an organizational structure could help absorb some of the internal conflict and change that newness and growth can bring. Being able to work issues through several layers of a board of trustees, administration, and key teachers and parents can help institutionalize the school and lend to healthy growth instead of dissatisfaction and school splits. Collaboration among school stakeholders, when made visible as initiated by the head of school, helps to mediate positive change and increase student outcomes. Administrators should also consider using a distributed leadership design to incorporate the concept of team leadership and joint decision making among school stakeholders. The use of evaluations and standard operating procedures should be considered and acknowledgement to the fine line that exists between empowerment of employees and impingement of initiative must be considered when creating school procedures and evaluations. Even before these policies are created, founders can expect to spend over 50 hours a week for as long as 8 months working on the new school project before opening the school. Reviewing the current student enrollment to maximum possible student enrollment can be a useful tool to quickly assess one, among many, factors of financial viability.

The Environment

Question 4 addressed the environment of the new start-up school. In particular this area addressed the relationship with the local bishop, the number of competing diocesan Catholic schools in the geographical area and the stability of the school board. This discussion will address the research question, "How does the relationship with the bishop and geographic location of the independent school affect its success"?

Relationship with the bishop. Eleven of the 17 schools responding to the survey are not recognized by the local bishop as Catholic (see Table 47), and one open school reported to have operated for 18 years before being asked by the bishop to seek official recognition (not initiating recognition on its own). Only one of the closed schools was recognized by the local bishop and included in the official Catholic directory. Overwhelmingly, recognition by the local bishop is not a fact of life for most NAPC*IS schools, even though their very existence is predicated on close adherence and obedience to the Catholic Church. Many NAPC*IS schools operate on the fringes of the diocesan structure surrounded by misconceptions and confusion as to what their relationship with the diocese and the Catholic Church really is. Some schools have been called "stepchildren" of the Catholic Church, a somewhat pejorative term used to undermine the initiative of lay faithful who have stepped forward to start a school in the Catholic tradition when one either did not exist, or in opposition to the explicit and perceived insensitivity of the diocesan school's teaching of human sexuality or other areas of Church teaching. Some dioceses make independent schools operating in the Catholic tradition wait 5 years before they can apply for recognition (McNiff, 1997). Once recognition is received a period of relationship building exists and a "testing of the waters" ensues where some mutual activities may or may not be performed. This researcher, as a private, independent Catholic high school founder, was invited to participate in diocesan administrator meetings and workshops. Collaboration within the diocesan structure allowed this researcher's school the opportunity to be included in diocesan website and newspaper advertisements. Through an exchange of skills and collaboration on mutually beneficial activities, one can gauge the relationship between the entities as either distant or close. In the open group of schools, what was statistically significant at the .01 level was the correlation between longevity and only formal communication with the diocese. Conversely, the longer the closed schools were open, the higher the correlation that some other type of communication with the diocese existed (see Table 57). More often than not, both the open and closed NAPC*IS schools were not included in diocesan advertising (66.7% for open schools and 80% for closed schools; see Table 48). There was no statistical significance between the diocese advertising the school and longevity (see Table 57) in the combined Spearman Rho analysis, although there was a statistically significant negative correlation (-.70, $p < .05$) between "diocese advertises school" and "longevity" in the open school group (see Table 58), indicating a high probability at the .05 level that the longer the school was open the more likely there was no advertising by the diocese of the school. Open schools seemed to operate successfully at an "arms-length" distance from the diocese with little mutual advertising. Official recognition by the diocese does not correlate at any degree of statistical significance in the combined group or when the groups were broken out into the open and closed groups.

Geographic location. Whether to open a private independent Catholic school adjacent to an existing diocesan school has always been a question for private school administrators. Are there enough students to support both schools? Will one school thrive and the other school fail because of pedagogy, curriculum, philosophy, or parent support?

Open schools, all of which incorporate elementary schools (see Table 40), reported operating with a substantial number of diocesan elementary schools existing within 45 minutes of their location (see Table 50). Three schools had a small number of competing elementary schools indicating between 0-5 schools. Four schools had between 6–10 and two schools reported between 11-20 competing schools. It is commendable for those schools to operate with competing schools that have almost similar missions within such close proximity. It was interesting to see that half of the respondents from open schools stated they had no idea how many students attended diocesan schools that were within a 45-minute drive of their current location. It would appear that this information would have high priority for administrators who are interested in attracting new students, especially since both business (Powers, 2012) and Catholic strategic planners (Meitler, 2012) use this information to plan new facilities. Perhaps the open private, independent schools are operating as "specialty" locations as discussed by Powers (2012). People tend to drive further for specialty "shops," even though schools would be considered everyday "commodities." Perhaps administrators are relying upon the uniqueness of their private schools to attract potential families and their concern for location is more situated around affordability and availability rather than competition with local diocesan schools. As reported by the founders or heads of school, the closed schools operated in an area that included few other diocesan elementary schools (see Table 50). This would indicate little competition for them since two of the closed schools were high schools and one was a PreK (see Table 40 and Table 41). They would not necessarily see these elementary schools as competition, but perhaps as feeder schools.

Open schools seem to have more diocesan high school competition within 45 minutes of their location (see Table 52). Fifty percent of the schools reported between 3-8 diocesan high schools existed within a 45 minute drive from their location. The closed schools did not have this amount of competition. Only 20% indicated there was between 3-5 diocesan high schools and no closed schools indicated there was between 6-8 diocesan high schools within 45 minutes. This is important to note because 9 of the 12 open schools incorporate Grades 9-12 in their grade level configuration (see Table 41).

Closed schools had information more about their competition based upon their responses concerning the number of elementary and high schools and the number of students in them than open schools who had a higher number of responses as "unknown" (see Tables 50-53).

Stability of school board. According to Guernsey and Barott (2008), private, independent Catholic schools have a high degree of disagreement between board members and this can affect the longevity of the school. Guernsey and Barott focused on the splitting off of board members and key school personnel from two different schools to start new private independent schools with very similar core missions and curriculum. When creating the NSRS for this research, it was suggested by a NAPC*IS school administrator to include a question regarding the stability of the board. The results from the survey indicated that this is indeed an area for concern as both the open and closed schools experienced instability within their school boards. Apparently, the open schools have worked through or are working through this instability. While this may be a reason for the closure of the other member schools, there is no empirical evidence to support this conclusion.

Conclusion and Summary

NAPC*IS schools are operating successfully within the geographical boundaries of competing diocesan elementary and high schools. This research indicated no statistically significant relationship between longevity of operations and official recognition by the bishop in the open school group. Many successful (open) NAPC*IS schools have only formal written communication with the diocese. This research indicates that the pursuit of recognition by the Catholic bishop should not be as important as the standardization of employee operating procedures and organizational design. While organizational design was included in the start-up category for this research based on the use of the Latham-Wexley method (Latham, Wexley, & Pursell, 1975) to ensure reliability and validity of survey design, it complements well with the components identified in the study of organizational decisions and considerations made by open and closed schools regarding employees following standard operating procedures, performance criteria and appraisals of employees, and a single person in command of the school. The variable of employees following standard operating procedure and longevity, within the organizational category, was the only variable that was statistically significant at $p < .01$. in the study. The other two variables of the use of performance criteria and appraisals and a single person in command of the school, both in the organizational category, were the third and fourth variables that indicated a fair degree of relationship to longevity, with incorporation of the school as the second variable that had a fair degree of relationship to longevity. Clearly, organizational issues at start-up and beyond should be key areas of interest for potential founders or entrepreneurs. Focusing on these types of organizational issues are more beneficial than what type of start-up procedures are used and would help with the institutionalization of the school if longevity is a major concern of the founders. Planning for the school is still important and founders should expect to put in an average of 7 months' of work before opening the school. Finding a school administrator with previous start-up experience or experience working in small business is not as important as finding someone with a master's degree or a minimum of 4 years of college. Finally, board instability is still an area of concern for open NAPC*IS schools.

Implications. From these results, successful private independent Catholic schools might expect to have only formal written communication between the bishop and the school and to operate independently, either as a complement, or alternative, to the existing diocesan school structure. Formal recognition as a Catholic school should not be the most important criteria aimed for in order to operate successfully, but stability of the school board remains an area in need of attention. Focusing on the organizational design, procedures, and future capacity building of employees is important. Start-up procedures should include incorporation, possibly with the use of an attorney. Successful schools in this study opened with $50,000 or less, with many founders or entrepreneurs contributing $20,000 or less to the school's operations.

Limitations

This small representation of closed schools cannot be generalized to the entire population of closed schools. This is unfortunate and a limitation of this study, although projection was not the intent of this research. As a nascent and understudied field, an explanatory observational approach was warranted to ferret out information about these schools that might stem the flow of closures and aid in the sustainability of current, and potential, new school start-ups.

Finding individuals to complete the survey from the closed schools was difficult. Only five schools from the total of 43 closed schools provided results for this survey. This small response can hardly generate a true picture of how these schools operate, their relationship to the bishop, and characteristics of their founders or procedures followed at start-up for all member schools. It is, though, a beginning, as no information from these closed schools has been quantitatively researched and analyzed.

Blending the two subject areas of entrepreneurship and private faith-based schools was a unique approach. Finding previously performed research in this combined area was almost non-existent. Most entrepreneurial research focused on business or industry and not educational organizations. Education in the United States has, until recently, been operated through local, state, and federal funding and not through the financing of individual entrepreneurs. With the charter movement we see the introduction of private for-profit and non-profit corporations into education. Private Catholic schools in the United States have primarily been operated by religious orders with donations from national and international sources and diocesan schools receive funding through local parish and system-wide diocesan efforts. It has only been within the last half century that private Catholic schools have sprung up, operated by the laity and funded primarily through tuition and grants from foundations and wealthy benefactors.

Another limitation of this study was the fact that little, to no research was available for those schools to build from, or to pull additional data from, except the research from Guernsey and Barott (2003). Their research was a qualitative study researching the split of two private independent schools into four schools and had a very narrow focus compared to the focus of this research which was to glean a comprehensive overview of components of successful NAPC*IS schools. This researcher had to go to other private faith-based research, such as research on the ACCS schools to use for comparison.

Further Research

This study was foundational in gleaning data about the founders of NAPC*IS schools, their start-up procedures, their organizational decisions, and the environment in which they opened, but the paucity of research and existing literature on these schools warrants additional analysis of the data received in this research, as well as other further quantitative and qualitative studies on these schools. While descriptive statistics delineated almost all of the results to the questions asked in the NSRS, the inferential statistics only focused on how each variable correlated to longevity, an indicator of success in this study. Further research can be performed using each of the variables in the four major categories as compared to other variables, both within the major categories and in each of the other categories. This analysis was outside of the focus of this research, but is worth future undertaking to glean some additional usable data regarding the successful schools.

While researching the many areas covered in this dissertation, from the decline of Catholic schools in the United States to types of leadership styles used by effective administrators in Catholic schools, so many questions were raised and additional opportunities for research were exposed. Recommendations for further research are as follows:

1. The faith leadership qualities of NAPC*IS school administrators should be compared to diocesan school administrators. What piqued this researcher's interest in this area was first reading a quote by Stravinskas' (2007) that stated, "never allow someone to declare that finances have been killing our (Catholic) (sic) schools; the crisis in confidence, the crisis in faith, has been doing them in" (p. 10). Was this "crisis in faith" really a reason for the closure of so many Catholic schools and did the founders of new private, independent Catholic schools possess that faith that leaders in the diocesan system lacked? When researching the area of educational background and knowledge of Catholic school principals, three sources of research-based data indicated that faith and spiritual leadership of administrators was an area of greatest need for development (Hines, 1999) or that leaders were inadequately prepared in this area for their leadership role (Schuttleoffel, 2003; Wallace, 1995). Superintendents in Hines' (1999) dissertation also indicated the greatest need for principals was the personal commitment to spirituality. Shuttleoffel's (2003) research showed that 71% of Catholic school administrations received leadership preparation in secular institutions (public colleges and universities) and that they lacked a formal spiritual preparation program, something that Shuttleoffel recommended after the study for implementation. It would be interesting to see what type of spiritual preparation NAPC*IS school founders have to assist them in their qualifications as spiritual leaders of their schools.

2. The evolution of the leadership approach and qualities of a leader regarding financial knowledge within NAPC*IS schools should be explored. As reported in the literature review above, leadership styles within schools have mirrored the newest leadership styles used in business and industry. While most of the open NAPC*IS schools included a broader base of constituencies in goal setting and day-to-day work activities following a distributed leadership pattern as opposed to a more autocratic one, is the mirroring of the latest business leadership style the most appropriate one for a school, and in particular a faith-based school? School literature on leadership distribution indicated that successful distribution of leadership happens when it was explicitly coordinated, planned, and initiated from the head of the school (Leithwood et al., 2009). In the evolution of leadership approaches, one can see the movement in industry to a leadership style based on the "lean" mindset cycle of the "build-measure-learn" feedback loop (Ries, 2011) of continuous improvement based on market demand and a quick, low cost, high quality customer response (Womack & Jones, 2003). Should NAPC*IS schools follow the Catholic school trend of adapting to the secular research as Walch (2001) stated has been the tradition of Catholic schools and which has kept them alive? Should NAPC*IS schools use business models and form their school leaders in areas of accounting, marketing, finance, human resources, and enrollment management advocated by Ozar (2010), Cimino (2010), and Nuzzi et al. (2013) for Catholic school leaders? Is

this adaptability of secularized initiatives something that NAPC*IS schools resist or are willing to accept?

3. What are the qualities of the open NAPC*IS schools that allow them to operate successfully alongside diocesan schools? What attracts students and families to choose these schools over diocesan schools and vice versa? Is it the curriculum, philosophy of education, class sizes, pedagogy, emphasis on the Catholic faith, extra-curricular that attract families and students to NAPC*IS schools? Is it the charisma of the leadership of the schools or the curriculum that attract families? What is it that is so unique about these schools that keep them operating in a highly competitive environment?

4. At what point after start-up have successful schools transferred leadership to other heads of schools or to a substantially new board and the transition from a personal school to an institutionalized one occurred? Questions such as "What are the succession plans for successful NAPC*IS schools?" "Do they exist?" "How have schools operating for 15 or more years made the transition, or transitions, to or through new leaders?" According to Guernsey and Barott (2008), leadership within NAPC*IS schools revolved substantially around power to control all aspects of the school, from curriculum and teaching to the purchase of new buildings. As these new ventures are so personally connected to their founders, how does the founder let go and what type of individual is required for this new phase of the school? Parker and Pragg (2010) looked at family businesses and family firm succession noting that only 30% of family businesses survive past the first generation. Would successive heads of school be considered in this category if the school has not taken steps to institutional, and what exactly does institutionalization mean? These are all very ripe areas for further research now that the initial floodgates have been opened by this research for more quantitative data mining.

Conclusion

To date, there has been very little research conducted on private independent Catholic schools in the United States although they have been in existence throughout the country for over 40 years. Only one other source of research on these schools was found (Guernsey & Barott, 2008). This researcher chose to take the unique approach of combining the areas of entrepreneurship and school research to glean factors of successful open NAPC*IS schools. In general, the successful open schools operate independently of the diocese with only formal written communication and in geographic areas where other diocesan schools exist. They are run by individuals who have advanced formal education and a moderate amount of full-time experience in the field of education, more supervisory experience, and small to no personal risk involved in the new start-up of the school. These individuals may, or may not, have previous start-up experience with other schools or businesses. Successful schools have, for the most part, opened without significant outside funding and some contact with potential families. Few alternatives were sought once the decision was made to move forward with the lead entrepreneur or founder investing anywhere from 28-34 hours per week toward the project in a span of under one year prior to school opening. Successful schools built the capacity of their personnel. From the time the schools opened, to the time of the survey, the skill sets of employees in successful schools expanded so that they were able to perform more roles within the school than when they were originally hired. They performed employee evaluations and had employees who performed standard operating procedures that were not as detailed as the closed schools. They used more distributed leadership by involving more of the school's stakeholders in more aspects of decision making. Founders of successful NAPC*IS schools spent well over 50 hours per week at the school during the first year of operation. Successful open schools had a higher ratio of current students served to possible students served per the O'Meara et al. (2013) ratio applied here to private independent Catholic schools.

It is important to keep in mind the characteristics of successful open NAPC*IS schools are based on a very small sample of schools and cannot be generalized to the entire population of NAPC*IS schools or to those schools outside of the association who are using a Catholic faith-based curriculum and are operating independently. It would be well worth the time to seek out those schools that are not part of the NAPC*IS school membership to learn the reasons for their existence. What was it that compelled them to open? Why are they operating independently? Are they "successful" schools according to the criteria of this research? Clearly, additional research opportunities exist for this still nascent and understudied category of schools.

References

Bellamy, G., Crawford, L., Marshall, L., & Coulter, G. (2005). The fail-safe schools challenge: Leadership possibilities from high reliability organizations. *Educational Administration Quarterly, 41*(3), 383-412. Retrieved from http://eaq.sagepub.com/content/41/3/383

Belmonte, A., & Cranston, N. (2009). The religious dimension of lay leadership in Catholic Schools: Preserving Catholic culture in an era of change. Catholic Education: *A Journal of Inquiry and Practice, 12*(3), 294-319.

Bolotta, A. (2012). The Catholic school principal as witness and servant leader: Building a living faith community by connecting vision to action. *Principal Connections, 15*(3), 6-10.

Boone, C., & Hendriks, W. (2009). Top management team diversity and firm performance: Moderators of functional-background and locus-of-control. *Management Science, 55*(2), 165-180.

Brinckmann, J., Grichnik, D., & Kapsa, D. (2010). Should entrepreneurs plan or just storm the castle? A meta-analysis on contextual factors impacting the business planning-performance relationship in small firms. *Journal of Business Venturing, 25*(1), 24-40. Retrieved from http://0-www.sciencedirect.com.novacat.nova.edu/ science/article/pii/S0883902608001109

Brockhaus, R. (1980). Risk taking propensity of entrepreneurs. *Academy of Management Journal, 23*, 509–520. Retrieved from http://search.proquest.com. ezproxylocal.library.nova.edu/docview/229512667/fulltextPDF/13B573899BB1D 41CFEA/1?accountid=6579

Castrogiovanni, G. (1996). Pre-startup planning and the survival of new small businesses: Theoretical linkages. *Journal of Management, 22*(6), 801-822.

Cimino, C. (2010). In search of the entrepreneurial leader. *Momentum, 41*(3), 6-8.

Clawson, J. (2012). *Level three leadership: Getting below the surface.* Upper Saddle River, NJ: Pearson Education.

David, J. (2010). What research says about…/Using value-added measures to evaluate teachers. *Educational Leadership, 67*(8), 81-82.

Diamond, D. (1987). *An analysis of leadership behavior and self-efficacy of principals of Catholic secondary schools.* Washington, DC: Catholic University of America.

Duchesneau, D. (1987). *New venture success in an emerging industry.* (Doctoral dissertation). Ft Lauderdale, FL: Nova Southeastern University.

Dygert, W. (2000). The president/principal model in Catholic secondary schools. *Catholic Education: A Journal of Inquiry and Practice, 4*(1), 16-41.

Fernald, L., Solomon, G., & Tarabishy, A. (2005). A new paradigm: Entrepreneurial leadership. *Southern Business Review, 30*(2), 1-10.

Fink, A. (2003). *How to manage, analyze, and interpret survey data* (2nd ed.). Thousand Oaks, CA: Sage Publications.

Frederickson, J., & Mitchell, T. (1984). Strategic decision processes: Comprehensiveness and performance in an industry with an unstable environment. *Academy of Management Journal, 27*, 399-423.

Gaudino, A. (2008). *Key issues in the teacher evaluation process of a Catholic school system: Implications for policy and practice.* Retrieved from http://d-scholarship.pitt.edu/6264/

Goodwin, B. (2013). Using teacher evaluation to avoid the "box of chocolates" syndrome. *Changing Schools, 68*, 10-12.

Gruber, M. (2007). Uncovering the value of planning in new venture creation: A process and contingency perspective. *Journal of Business Venturing, 22*, 782-807.

Guernsey, D., & Barott, J. (2008). Conflict in independent Catholic schools. *Catholic Education: A Journal of Inquiry and Practice, 11*(4). Retrieved from http://ejournals.bc.edu/ojs/index.php/catholic/article/view/1034

Hines, E. (1999). *The perception of lay Catholic elementary school principals and superintendents of the faith formation of principals.* Retrieved from http://search.proquest.com.ezproxylocal.library.nova.edu/pqdtft/docview/3045819
52/abstract/13BAE9C86A6428C81AC/1?accountid=6579

Iannaccone, L. (1983). Community education and turning point election periods (TPEPs). In D. H. Schoeny & L. E. Decker (Eds.), *Community, educational and social impact perspectives* (pp. 105-115). Charlottesville, VA: University of Virginia.

Kane, T., & Cantrell, S. (2012). *Learning about teaching: Initial findings from the measures of effective teaching project.* Seattle, WA: Bill and Melinda Gates Foundation.

Kealey, R. (Ed.). (1997). *Opening a new Catholic school: A series of case studies.* Washington, DC: National Catholic Educational Association.

Kennedy, S. (2012). *Building 21st century Catholic learning communities: enhancing the Catholic mission with data, blended learning, and other best practices from top charter schools.* Arlington, VA: Lexington Institute.

Kessler, A., & Frank, H. (2009). Nascent entrepreneurship in a longitudinal perspective. *International Small Business Journal, 27*(6), 720-742. doi:10.1177/0266242609344363

Kim, P., Aldrich, H., & Keister, L. (2003). *If I were rich? The impact of financial and human capital on becoming a nascent entrepreneur.* Retrieved from http://www.allacademic.com/meta/p107958_index.html

Lange, J., Mollov, A., Pearlmutter, M., Singh, S., & Bygrave, W. (2007). Pre-start-up formal business plans and post-start-up performance: A study of 116 new ventures. *Venture Capital, 9*(4), 237-256. doi:10.1080/13691060701414840

Latham, G., Wexley, K., & Pursell, E. (1975). Training managers to minimize rating errors in the observation of behavior. *Journal of Applied Psychology, 60*(7), 550-555.

Leithwood, K., Day, C., Sammons, P., Harris, A., & Hopkins, D. (2007). *Leadership and student learning outcomes, Interim report.* London, England: DCSF.

March, J., & Simon, H. (1958). *Organizations.* New York, NY: John Wiley & Sons.

Marshall, K. (2012). Fine-tuning teacher evaluations. *Educational Leadership, 70*(3), 50-53.

McDonald, D., & Schultz, M. (2011). *United States Catholic elementary and secondary schools 2009-2010: The annual statistical report on schools, enrollment and staffing.* Retrieved from http://www.ncea.org/news/AnnualDataReport.asp

McNiff, T. (1997). Procedures for opening a new school-Diocese of Arlington, VA. In R. Kealey (Ed.), *Opening a new Catholic School: A series of case studies* (pp.1-8). Washington, DC: National Catholic Educational Association.

Meitler. (2012). *Demographics and market research: Success stories, Diocese of Ft. Worth.* Retrieved from http://www.meitler.com/services/demographics-market-research/

Miner, J., & Raju, N. (2004). Risk propensity differences between managers and entrepreneurs and between low-and-high growth entrepreneurs: A reply in a more conservative nein. *Journal of Applied Psychology, 89,* 313.

National Association of Private Catholic and Independent Schools. (2013a). *Find a school.* Retrieved from http://www.napcis.org

National Association of Private Catholic and Independent Schools. (2013b). *NAPC*IS feasibility manual.* Sacramento, CA: NAPC*IS.

National Catholic Education Association. (2011). *Brief overview of Catholic schools in America.* Retrieved from http://www.ncea.org/about/HistoricalOverview ofCatholicSchoolsInAmerica.asp?print=y

Nuzzi, R., Holter, A., & Frabutt, J. (2013). *Striving for balance, steadfast in faith: The Notre Dame study of U.S. Catholic elementary school principals.* Charlotte, NC: Information Age Publishing, Inc.

O'Meara, Ferguson, Whelan, & Conway, Inc. (2012). *Revitalizing Catholic schools: Alternative analysis and solutions for Catholic schools.* Retrieved from http://www.omearaferguson.com/files/RevitalizingCatholicSchools.pdf

Ozar, L. (2010). A new generation of leaders for a new generation of schools. *Momentum, 41*(4), 6–7.

Ozar, L., Boland, M., Carriere, W., Dinger, W., Herb, J., O'Block, et al. (2012). *National standards and benchmarks for effective Catholic elementary and secondary schools.* Retrieved from http://www.catholicschool standards.org

Parker, S., & Praag, M. (2010). The entrepreneur's mode of entry: Business takeover or new venture start? *Journal of Business Venturing.* doi:10.1016/j.jbusvent. 2010.08.002

Pines, A., Dvir, D., & Sadeh, A. (2012). Dispositional antecedents, job correlates and performance outcomes of entrepreneurs" risk taking. *International Journal of Entrepreneurship, 16.* Retrieved from http://www.freepatentsonline.com/ article/International-Journal-Entrepreneurship/289620969.html

Powers, T. (2012). Early schools of marketing thought and marketplace evolution. *Journal of Historical Research in Marketing, 4*(1), 190–206. doi.org/10.1108/17557501211195127

Reynolds, P., & Curtin, R. (2008). Business creation in the United States: Panel study of entrepreneurial dynamics II initial assessment. *Foundation and Trends in Entrepreneurship, 4*(3), 155–307.

Ries, E. (2011). *The lean start-up: How today's entrepreneurs use continuous innovation to create radically successful businesses.* New York, NY: Crown Publishing Group.

Ronstadt, R. (1984). *Entrepreneurship.* Dover, MA: Lord Publishing.

Schuttloffel, M. (2003). *Report on the future of Catholic school leadership.* Washington, DC: National Catholic Educational Association.

Stewart, V. (2013). School leadership around the world. *Educational Leadership 70*(7), 48-54.

Stravinskas, P. (2007). Catholic schools in perspective. *Catholic Educator, 2*(Spring), 6-10.

U.S. Department of Education, National Center for Education Statistics. (2011). *Enrollment in elementary and secondary schools, by control and level of Institution: Selected years, fall 1970 through fall 2019.* Retrieved from http://nces.ed.gov/fastfacts/display.asp?id=65

Van de Ven, A., Hudson, R., & Schroeder, D. (1984). Designing new business startups: Entrepreneurial, organizational, and ecological considerations. *Journal of Management, 10*(1), 87-107.

Van de Ven, A., & Koenig, R. (1976). A process model for program planning and evaluation. *Journal of Economics and Business, 28* (3), 161-170.

Varlas, L. (2012). Rethinking teacher evaluation: Leaders advocate for more meaningful measures. *Educational Leadership, 54*(12), 1-6.

Wadhwa, V., Aggarwal, R., Holly, K., & Salkever, A. (2009). *The anatomy of an entrepreneur: Making of a successful entrepreneur.* Kansas City, MO: Kauffman Foundation.

Walch, T. (2001). The past is prologue: American Catholic education and the new century. *Catholic education: A journal of inquiry and practice, 4*(3), 355-363.

Wallace, T. (1995). *Assessment of the preparedness of lay Catholic high school principals to be faith leaders.* Retrieved from http://search.proquest.com.ezproxylocal.library.nova.edu/pqdtft/docview/3042633 83/abstract/13BAE9DA82F709AE057/1?accountid=6579

Williams, J., McKinney, C., Garland, R., & Goodwin, B. (2010). How North Carolina improved teacher evaluation. *Educational Leadership, 67*(8). Retrieved from http:// www.ascd.org/publications/educational-leadership/may10/vol67/num08/How-North-Carolina-Improved-Teacher-Evaluation.aspx

Womack, J. & Jones, D. (2003). *Lean thinking: Banish waste and create wealth in your corporation.* New York, NY: Free Press.

Yeager, R., Benson, P., Guerra, M., & Manno, B. (1985). *The Catholic high school: A national portrait.* Washington, DC: National Catholic Educational Association.

Appendix A

Comparison of Start-Up Procedures

	Start-Up Processes for Schools Compared to the Program Planning Model							
	Meitler School & Parish	NCEA	Association of Classical	Classical				
		Diocese of		School	Private*		Small	Total
Component of Start Up	Consulting	Arlington	Christian Sch.	Garfield	(general)	NAPC*IS	public	similar
	Web site 2012	1997	(ACCS) 2005	1996	Web site 2012	2013	1997	category
Program Planning Model								
Problem identification (1)	X (1)							1
Data gathering & Analysis (2)	X (2)	X (informal) (3)	X (informal) (6)	X (1)				4
Alternatives & Options (3)	X (3)							1
Professionals involved (3)	X (3)	X (a)			X(2)	X (15)		4
Inclusion of Client base (4)	X (4)		X (15)		X (2)		X (9)	4
Formal Business Plan (4)	X (4)				X (4)			2
Small Scale Activatiaon (5)	X (model)							1
Full Scale Activation (6)	X (6)							1
Evaluation (7)	X (5 years)						X (15)	2
Approvals								
Desire of the pastor		X (1)						1
Acknowledgement of								
Policies & Guidelines		X (2)						1
Diocesan School Board Approval		X (4)						1
Opinions of surrounding pastors		X (5)						1
Diocesan Finance Approval		X (8)						1
Catechetical approval		X (9)						1
Spiritual								
Prayer & Sacraments			X (1)			X (1)		2
Adoration & Sacraments						X (2)		1
Prayers from others						X (3)		1
Spiritual Advisor						X (4)		1
Founding Statements								
Purpose/Motive				X (1)				1
Mission				X (6)		X (5)		2
Vision			X (3)	X (2)			X (1)	3

Philosophy ,Goals, Objectives				X (7)				1
Governance								
Core Committee				X (3)	X (2)			2
Governance			X (2)	X (4)		X (6)	X (8)	4
Oath of Fidelity by Board Members						X (7)		1
Statement of Faith			X (4)					1
Job Description of Board Members						X (12)		1
Establish relationship w/Bishop						X (17)		1
Legal								
Incorporation			X (5)		X(3)	X (9)		3
Obtain Fed. EIN#						X (10)		1
IRS tax exemption					X(3)	X (11)		2
Legal req. facility			X (11)		X(7)	X (24)		3
Legal req. Health & Safety			X (11)		X (7)	X (24)		3
Financial								
5 year budget - operating					X (5)			1
5 year budget - captial					X (5)			1
1 year budget		X (6)		X (15)			X (13)	3
Facility			X (12)	X (15)	X (7)		X (14)	4
Ability to Fund		X (7)						1
$250 deposit by founders*						X (8)		1
Fundraising & Development								
Fundraising Committee			X (13)		X (6)	X (27)		3
Development Office			X (18)	X (14)				2
Human Resource								
Hire Head of School:			X (9)					1
Self Starter					X (8)			1
Male				X (10)				1
character, profes., vision, prayful/Founder						X (13)		1
Hire Business Manager					X (12)			1
Hire Faculty:			X (10)	X (11)			X (7)	3
"skilled"					X (11)			1
"apostle, professional, kind"						X (19)		1
Job Descriptions/Lines of Authority				X (9)	X (8)			2

Marketing							
Advertise		X (19)	X (12)	X (9)			3
Student recruitment				X (10)	X (18)	X (3)	3
Communications						X (11)	1
Operations							
Determine grades served		X (8)	X (8)	X (2)		X (2)	4
Start small				X (3)	X (25)		2
Set an Opening Date					X (14)		1
Observe 2 - 3 small schools					X (16)		1
Begin operation		X (14)		X (10)			2
Train faculty/Prof. Dev.		X (16)		X (12)		X (10)	3
Join Associations			X (5)	X (13)			2
Outline Administrative Procedures			X (13)		X (21)	X (4)	3
Outline Curriculum & Instruction		X (7)	X (13)		X (20)	X (5)	4
Assessment practices		X (17)				X (6)	2
Scheduling						X (12)	1
Discipline Policy					X (22)		1
Stay Small					X (26)		1
Accreditation		X (20)			X(24)		2
Policy Handbooks					X (23)		

(a)	(b)
School Board	Finance
Finance Committee	Legal
Construction Experts	Management
Catechists	Real Estate
	Other paid talent
	* Halladay education Group
	Robert Kennedy, Starting a private school

Halliday Eduction Group Inc. (2012). *13 step school formation model*.

Retrieved from www.halladayeduationgroup.com/files/reports/13-step_school_formation_model.pdf

Kennedy, R. (2012). *Starting a private school.*

Retrieved from http://privateschool.about.com/cs/start ingaschool/ht/startaschool.htm								

* $250 Good Faith Estimate is both a personal and practical commitment, per Eileen Cubanski (personal communication, January 7, 2013)

Appendix B
NAPC*IS School Research Survey

NAPC*IS School Research Survey

Directions:
Please answer the following questions in the space provided.
Place an "X" for the selected response.

1.1 – The Individual

1.101   Before starting this school, how much full-time experience did you have in the field of education?

    1 = [   ] 0
    2 = [   ] 1-5 yrs.
    3 = [   ] 6-10 yrs.
    4 = [   ] 11-15 yrs.
    5 = [   ] 16 and above

1.102   Before starting this school, how many years did you work in a small business?

    1 = [   ] 0
    2 = [   ] 1-5 yrs.
    3 = [   ] 6-10 yrs.
    4 = [   ] 11-15 yrs.
    5 = [   ] 16 and above

1.103   In a leadership capacity, what was the largest number of people who regularly reported to you in a business, military, educational, professional or other organization?

    1 = [   ] 2 or less
    2 = [   ] 3 to 10
    3 = [   ] 11 to 50
    4 = [   ] 51 to 250
    5 = [   ] over 250

1.104   Prior to this school start-up, did you start up any other businesses?

    1 = [   ] 0 businesses
    2 = [   ] 1-2 businesses
    3 = [   ] 3-4 businesses
    4 = [   ] 5-6 businesses
    5 = [   ] 7 or more businesses

1.105   How great did you see your personal risk if this business/school failed?

    1 = [   ] None or practically none
    2 = [   ] Small
    3 = [   ] Some
    4 = [   ] Great
    5 = [   ] Catastrophic

1.106   What was the approximate amount of your personal investment in this business (personal cash and/or personal borrowings)?

     1 = [   ] $0 - $1,000
     2 = [   ] $1,001 - $20,000
     3 = [   ] $20,001 - $40,000
     4 = [   ] $40,001 - $60,000
     5 = [   ] $60,001 and above

1.107   What is the highest level of education you have reached?

     1 = [   ] High school or less (# years 1-12)
     2 = [   ] 1-3 years college (# years 13-17)
     3 = [   ] 4 years degree (# years 16)
     4 = [   ] Masters or other post graduate degree (# years 18)
     5 = [   ] Doctoral degree (# years 20)

1.2 – Start – Up Procedures

1.201a   Did you have:

     1 = [   ] No contact with potential families and no market analysis
     2 = [   ] Very small or limited amount of contact with potential families or market analysts.
     3 = [   ] Some contact with potential families and market analysis
     4 = [   ] Substantial contact with potential families or market analysis
     5 = [   ] Extensive and comprehensive contact with potential families or market analysts.

1.201b   To what degree were alternate ways and potential means explored in responding to market needs?

     1 = [   ] No alternate ways or potential means were explored.
     2 = [   ] Very few, or very limited alternatives and potential means were explored.
     3 = [   ] Some alternative ways and potential means were explored.
     4 = [   ] A substantial number of alternate ways and means were explored.
     5 = [   ] A great number of alternate ways and means were explored.

1.202   Overall, at start-up, how many weeks and hours per week were spent in planning this school?

[   ] # of weeks **X** [   ] average hours per week = [   ] Total # of hours

1.203   To what degree were potential families involved during the early planning stages of your business, prior to the start–up?

     1 = [   ] Not at all
     2 = [   ] A little
     3 = [   ] To some degree

4 = [   ] Substantially involved
5 = [   ] Greatly involved

1.204   To what degree were professionals such as consultants, lawyers, accountants, etc. involved in the development of your business plan?

1 = [   ] Not at all
2 = [   ] A little
3 = [   ] To some degree
4 = [   ] Substantially involved
5 = [   ] Greatly involved

At start-up, did you…

1.204a   Use an attorney?   1 = No [   ]   2 = Yes [   ]

1.204b   Use an accountant?   1 = No [   ]   2 = Yes [   ]

1.204c   Use an architect?   1 = No [   ]   2 = Yes [   ]

1.204d   Use a banker?   1 = No [   ]   2 = Yes [   ]

1.205a   Did you develop a formal written business plan prior to the start – up of the school?

1 = No [   ]   2 = Yes [   ]

1.205b   Did you use written notes or records for planning the start – up of the school?

1 = No [   ]   2 = Yes [   ]

1.205c   Indicate any areas covered in the written notes or business plan that you used at start-up:

a.   1=[   ] No.   2=[   ] Yes.   A. incorporation
b.   1=[   ] No   2=[   ] Yes.   B. marketing
c.   1=[   ] No.   2=[   ] Yes.   C. financial needs and sources
d.   1=[   ] No.   2=[   ] Yes.   D. pro-forma bal. sheet, income stmt
e.   1=[   ] No.   2=[   ] Yes.   E. facility needs and sources
f.   1=[   ] No.   2=[   ] Yes.   F. personnel needs
g.   1=[   ] No.   2=[   ] Yes.   G. organizational design
h.   1=[   ] No.   2=[   ] Yes.   H. client base
i.   How many persons did you send your written business plan to?
         1=[   ] No one
         2=[   ] 1 person
         3=[   ] 2 or 3 persons
         4=[   ] 4 persons
         5=[   ] 5 or more persons

1.206 At start up, how much funding was received by an outside source (i.e., foundation, philanthropist)?

  1 = [ ] $0 - $50,000
  2 = [ ] $50,001 - $100,000
  3 = [ ] $100,001 - $150,000
  4 = [ ] $150,001 - $200,000
  5 = [ ] $200,001 – and above

1.3 – Organization

1.301a How many hired employees were qualified to fill more than their current position at school opening? For example: teaching and administrating

  1 = [ ] None are qualified
  2 = [ ] Few are qualified
  3 = [ ] About half are qualified
  4 = [ ] Many are qualified
  5 = [ ] All or nearly all are qualified

1.301b How many employees were/are qualified to fill more than their current position today, or at closing? For example: teaching and administrating

  1 = [ ] None are qualified
  2 = [ ] Few are qualified
  3 = [ ] About half are qualified
  4 = [ ] Many are qualified
  5 = [ ] All or nearly all are qualified

1.302 To what extent do hired employees in this school follow standard operating procedures or policies to do their job?

  1 = [ ] Not at all.
  2 = [ ] To a small extent
  3 = [ ] To some extent
  4 = [ ] To a substantial extent
  5 = [ ] To a great extent

1.303 How detailed are these standardized operating procedures in defining the way in which work and work activities are to be done?

  1 = [ ] Very general
  2 = [ ] Mostly general
  3 = [ ] Somewhat specific
  4 = [ ] Quite specific
  5 = [ ] Very specific

1.304   To what extent are performance criteria and appraisal procedures established to evaluate the work of people in this school?

1 = [   ] Not at all
2 = [   ] To a small extent
3 = [   ] To some extent
4 = [   ] To a substantial extent
5 = [   ] To a great extent

1.305   To what degree is there a single person in command of this school?

1 = [   ] To no extent
2 = [   ] To a small extent
3 = [   ] To some extent
4 = [   ] To a substantial extent
5 = [   ] To a great extent

1.306   To what degree has the school founder/lead entrepreneur allowed Board members, other administrators, and teachers to be involved in making decisions on developing goals and strategies for the school?

	a.) Board members	b.) Administrators	c.) Teachers
1 = None	[ ]	[ ]	[ ]
2 = A little	[ ]	[ ]	[ ]
3 = Somewhat	[ ]	[ ]	[ ]
4 = Quite a bit	[ ]	[ ]	[ ]
5 = Very much	[ ]	[ ]	[ ]

1.307   To what degree have Board members, administrators and teachers been involved in making decisions on how work activities are to be performed in the school?

	a.) Board members	b.) Administrators	c.) Teachers
1 = None	[ ]	[ ]	[ ]
2 = A little	[ ]	[ ]	[ ]
3 = Somewhat	[ ]	[ ]	[ ]
4 = Quite a bit	[ ]	[ ]	[ ]
5 = Very much	[ ]	[ ]	[ ]

1.308a   Compared to the other administrators in the organization, how many total hours did the lead entrepreneur (Founder) work during the first year following the opening of the school?

1 = [   ] 40 hours or less per week
2 = [   ] Over 41 hours to 50 hours per week
3 = [   ] Over 51 but less than 60 hours per week
4 = [   ] Over 60 but less than 70 hours per week
5 = [   ] Over 70 hours per week

1.308b   Compared to the other administrators in the organization, how many total hours did the lead entrepreneur (Founder) work during the past 6 months (or last 6 month prior to closing)?

        1 = [   ] 40 hours or less per week
        2 = [   ] Over 41 hours to 50 hours per week
        3 = [   ] Over 51 but less than 60 hours per week
        4 = [   ] Over 60 but less than 70 hours per week
        5 = [   ] Over 70 hours per week

1.308c   On the average, how many total hours did the lead entrepreneur (Founder) work at another part-time or full-time job (other than the school) during the first year following the start up of the school?

        1 = [   ] 40 hours or less per week
        2 = [   ] Over 41 hours to 50 hours per week
        3 = [   ] Over 51 but less than 60 hours per week
        4 = [   ] Over 60 but less than 70 hours per week
        5 = [   ] Over 70 hours per week

1.309   During the last year (or last year of operation), how much funding did your organization (school) receive from outside sources such as foundation and philanthropists?

        1 = [   ] $0 - $50,000
        2 = [   ] $50,001 - $100,000
        3 = [   ] $100,001 - $150,000
        4 = [   ] $150,001 - $200,000
        5 = [   ] $200,001 – and above

1.310   What is your current (or at closing) annual operating budget?

        1 = [   ] under $100,000
        2 = [   ] $100,001 - $200,000
        3 = [   ] $200,001 - $300,000
        4 = [   ] $300,001 - $400,000
        5 = [   ] $400,001 – and above

1.311   What grade levels do/did you serve?

        1 = [   ] K-6 (or fewer grades)
        2 = [   ] K-8
        3 = [   ] 7-12
        4 = [   ] 9-12
        5 = [   ] Other configuration

1.312   How many students do you serve today (or last month open)? _____

1.313   How many students are (were) you capable of serving at your facility?

       _____

1.314   How many months has/was this school open? _____ # months

1.4 – The Environment

1.401   This school is/was recognized by the Bishop of the Diocese as an official "Catholic" school and is included in the official Catholic Directory.

1 = [   ] Yes
2 = [   ] No

1.402   The local Diocese supports/ed the school advertising it alongside other Diocesan schools in the local Diocesan newspaper.

1 = [   ] Yes
2 = [   ] No

1.403   There is/was only formal written communication between the Diocesan offices and the school.

1 = [   ] Yes
2 = [   ] No

1.404a   How many Catholic (Diocesan recognized) elementary schools (K-6 or K-8) are/were within 45 minutes of your school? _____ #

1.404b   Approximate number of schoolchildren who attend or attended these schools.

_____ #

1.405a   How many Catholic (Diocesan recognized) high schools are/were within 45 minutes of your school?

_____ #

1.405b   Approximate number of schoolchildren who attend/ed these high schools.

_____ #

1.406a   Percentage of Catholic students upon school opening _____ %

1.406b   Percentage of Catholic students currently (or at closing) _____ %

1.407   What is the City and State of you school? _____

1   2   3   4
(Circle 1 = Eastern time, 2 = Central time, 3 = Mountain time, 4 Western time

1.408   The School Board has remained relatively stable over the years (few changes of Board members).

1 = [   ] Yes
2 = [   ] No

1.5 – Other Items

1.501   Please list any other items that you feel might be helpful to identify what components of success you feel are necessary to sustain private Catholic independent schools.

_____

_____

_____

Thank you for participating in this very important survey. Upon receipt of your survey, you will receive a $10 amazon gift certificate and your email address will be placed in a drawing to win an additional $100 Amazon gift certificate.

Made in United States
North Haven, CT
13 May 2022

19137143R00052